AFTER THE STORM

A BETTER LIFE BEYOND COVID

Testimonials for Brian Morgan and his work

Tributes have flowed to Brian Morgan for fifty years. Here are a few excerpts about earlier work:

Trust Brian Morgan. He has touched the depths of life and climbed the tree of wisdom. His motives are authentic and his heart is an open book. *Henrietta Falsom, journalist, reviewer.*

Your work is going to be an amazing blessing to the world... It is a rare topic... You are actually resolving a big problem. [People who have to cope with isolation and solitude] will now have a reference point. Thank you for doing the work. *Pastor Sunday Adelaja, sundayadelajablog.com.*

I should have expected something like this from you, Brian. You are an inspiration on social media and a constant friend to everyone who wants a hand. Thank you. *William Fitzhenry, writer/reviewer.*

The world thanks you for your life-changing stories. *Antoinette-Schokman de Silva, writer on LinkedIn.*

Sounds to me like you balanced your life beautifully, Brian. Striking this balance is the key to the fulfilling life people are looking for in today's world... Getting clear on what success means to you leads to deep-rooted joy. *Maria Gavriel, coach/author/speaker.*

Brian, you are right - we love challenges! You are an inspiration to many of us! *Thierry Coridon Jeremie, Cyprus.*

Thanks for those lovely and inspiring words Brian. We are like souls... trying to leave a footprint or two behind. *Carl Delprat, writer/artist/reviewer.*

I got fascinated when I read your LI profile, and it showed that you could help us. Thank you so much... I am inspired by all the brilliant works you have been doing. *Peter Deng, Africa World Books.*

Congratulations on your joining the Global Goodwill Ambassador family, it will be great to have a person of your calibre with us, in helping the world to take at least one step higher than what it is now. *Quintus Andradi.*

... Brian's mind was elsewhere – on the writing he was quietly practising in his head and on paper. And he gradually came to understand that he could combine the knowledge he had accumulated with the moral code he had developed, and he could help others with this recipe of skill and integrity... *The Writers Trust.*

Before you buy and read and learn and gain inspiration from what he writes, read the resume of the author, an accomplished business and thought leader, a professional writer and an accomplished teacher, who clearly has applied the principles he has used to drive his own successful career and his own life. Then open the pages and be transported... as he eloquently illustrates how and why some things and some values never vary. *The Richest Man in Persia* shall remain, with its many bookmarks and dog-eared pages, on my bookshelf. *Don Darkes, author of 6692 - Pisces the Sailfish.*

A very accomplished piece of writing that absorbed the reader throughout. Polished in style and execution. Seamless. A captivating journey back in time. *Archimede Fusillo, author and judge of the FAW Jim Hamilton Award.*

Good books are always in demand, especially if they are well written and the premise is sound and logical, as yours is. Your style is beautifully polished and easy to read. *Vera Thompson, editor and book publisher.*

The first thing I have to say is that Brian Morgan's work is written from the heart. He has an international reputation for his work – and this will add to the accolades. Most of the book is from Brian Morgan's own magical pen, but it draws from others as well to create what the cover promises. *James Barrett, journalist and reviewer.*

I don't write reviews for books, but this one deserves to be told. I just loved it. I think Brian Morgan has a beautiful way with words and his heart shows in the beautiful things he wrote... This book will lift you and touch you and make you think in a different way. Just gorgeous. *Mary-Ann Tully, reader.*

I have to say it is one of the very best books I have read for a long time. Brian gets to the heart of ethics in an original and compelling way. I found this to be not only helpful but entertaining, while making very clear, in plain and simple terms, some vital truths. The way of life suggested would benefit everyone. *Vivienne Edwards.*

Bonus Reading

This book comes with two bonus stories. The author has called them both epilogues, because they both relate to and enhance *After the Storm*.

The first epilogue tells the story of a beautiful poem, *Desiderata,* which has captivated hearts around the world for many years.

It's the story of one man and his effort to come out of tough times and create a better life for himself – much as we want to do during and after this COVID-19 pandemic.

The full poem, of course, is included.

The second epilogue tells the story of a small nation of people who were facing death and struggling to survive in a terrible place at a terrible time.

The nation's wisdom-keepers thought up ways to lift spirits, to face insurmountable odds and to find peace and serenity in a cruel world.

Isn't that something that might help us as we seek a better life for ourselves and our families?

We hope you enjoy the book and the two stories that accompany it.

The Writers Trust. October 2020.

AFTER THE STORM

A BETTER LIFE BEYOND COVID

BRIAN MORGAN

THE WRITERS TRUST
Sydney and The Central Coast, NSW, Australia

"Life is so transient and ephemeral; we will not be here after a breath.
So think better, think deeply, think with kindness,
and write it with love so that it may live a little longer."
Debasish Mridha

֍֍֍

This first edition paperback is published for world-wide distribution by The Writers Trust in 2020. This book is associated with the author's website at www.brianmorganbooks.com.

The author and publisher gratefully acknowledge the thoughts and brilliance of the writers and others whose words and ideas enrich this book. Epigrams for each chapter are by the named writers.

Some passages of this book first appeared in several of Brian Morgan's other books, particularly *You Are Already Rich,* published by The Writers Trust.

Produced by KDP Amazon for the publisher and available through Amazon online stores. Simply search for the full title of the book.

ISBN: 978-0-6485147-1-8

THE WRITERS TRUST

Sydney and the Central Coast, NSW, Australia.

DEDICATION

For all those who have suffered through the COVID-19 pandemic. For the many heroes of the pandemic – the doctors and nurses and others who worked beyond exhaustion to care for the sick; and for the multitudes of extraordinary people who also worked at the risk of their own health to help others – the drivers, cleaners, retail staff, police, paramedics, teachers and so many others.

You know who you are.

The world is forever in your debt.

And to your family and mine as we seek
a better life beyond the pandemic.
Bless you all.

May our next pandemic be one of
kindness and peace of mind.

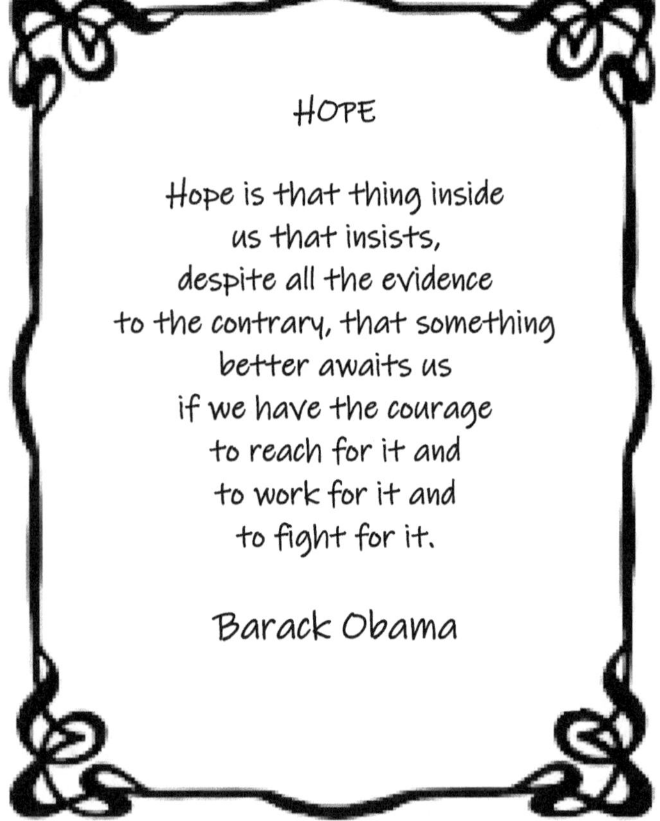

HOPE

Hope is that thing inside
us that insists,
despite all the evidence
to the contrary, that something
better awaits us
if we have the courage
to reach for it and
to work for it and
to fight for it.

Barack Obama

Contents

The best we can hope for
in this life is
a knothole peek at the
shining realities ahead.
Yet a glimpse is enough.
It's enough to convince our
hearts that whatever
sufferings and sorrows
currently assail us
aren't worthy of
comparison to that which
waits over the horizon.

Joni Eareckson Tada

The Wrath of the Gods

"Courage is resistance to fear, mastery of fear - not absence of fear."
Mark Twain

"When we least expect it, life sets us a challenge to test our courage and willingness to change. At such a moment, there is no point in pretending that nothing has happened or in saying that we are not yet ready. The challenge will not wait. Life does not look back. A week is more than enough time for us to decide whether or not to accept our destiny."
Paulo Coelho

"There is strange comfort in knowing that no matter what happens today, the Sun will rise again tomorrow."
Aaron Lauritsen

For more than a thousand years of recorded history, the hapless inhabitants of Planet Earth have periodically suffered plagues and pandemics that have smashed civilisations and killed millions of people.

The trail of misery reached every continent and every corner of the globe. People in every village and every town wept for ruined lives, destroyed families and broken hearts.

Long ago, when people were defenceless against disease, they said it was the wrath of the Gods. These days we struggle to make sense of it and explain it to our children.

The Bubonic Plague, Smallpox, the Spanish Flu, the Plague of Justinian, HIV/AIDS and influenza have been some of the most brutal killers this world has seen. They have been merciless. They have slain hundreds of millions of helpless victims.

Disease has been a greater killer than war.

The Bubonic Plague (The Black Death) slaughtered more than 200 million and wiped out almost half of Europe's population.

It took more than 200 years for the continent to recover.

Smallpox, which raged for centuries into our own time, killed an estimated 90 percent of the Native American population and, during part of the 1800s, 400,000 Europeans died each year.

Historians believe the Plague of Justinian hastened the fall of the Roman Empire. In our lifetime, 35 million people died of HIV/AIDS in 40 years.

And then came COVID

As this book is written, COVID-19 is wreaking havoc and misery in more than 200 countries on every continent.

In December 2019, in the Wuhan region of China, a new ("novel") coronavirus began appearing in stunned human beings. COVID-19 is a shortened form of "coronavirus disease of 2019."

This virus spread extremely quickly between people because it was new. No-one on Earth was immune because no-one had had it before.

COVID-19 began as an epidemic in China, but spread worldwide within months. The World Health Organisation declared COVID-19 a pandemic in March 2020.

A pandemic (from the Greek pan, "all", and demos, "people") is an epidemic that has spread over a wide region and affected a substantial number of people.

By March, more than a half-million people had been infected and 30,000 had died. By September, more than 30 million had been infected and a million had died. But the World Health Organisation believed the real figures would show one in ten people on the planet infected.

The outcome of the COVID-19 pandemic is impossible to predict at the time of this writing. But we can learn from pandemics in history, and have done so. They are our teachers.

Fever to stop a fever

Laboratories and universities around the world are working feverishly, using this knowledge base and new technology, to find treatments for symptoms and vaccines to provide immunity in the community to hit back at this disease.

The push for the human race to survive this pandemic has become the primary focus around the world.

A virus cannot be seen, and it's usually the unseen that provokes terror in the imagination. The end of this pandemic is unknown. The future uncertain, at best.

However, thanks largely to the medical profession and scientists around the world, there's one consistent trend over time – a gradual reduction in the death rate from disease.

That medical profession is now stretched to the limit. We've seen pictures of health workers at the end of their long shifts. We won't forget them. Doctors, nurses and volunteers all exhausted, faces blotched and red where masks and protective gear have marked their skin.

And their eyes. Those eyes have seen too much.

We, most of us, could only do what we were asked to do and try to make things easier for these caring heroes.

We did what we could, from hand-washing to social distancing. Countries declared compulsory stay-at-home measures, closing schools, businesses and public places. We didn't like it, but most of us did what we could.

This social-distancing strategy was working, but at such an economic cost that it could not be sustained indefinitely. Experts feared that, when restrictions relaxed, the coronavirus would likely surge back.

It did.

Nobody wrote the manual

Some are saying that it will be at least two years before we can even think of things getting back to "normal". We have never faced a pandemic like this in modern times, so there's no manual and too many unknown answers. We just don't know yet how to move forward.

Those seeking answers are saying we need to understand that this will be part of our lives for a long time. There will be no quick or decisive victory.

I'm no expert, but I have been a keen observer of this world for a long time and I think we have to make peace with the idea that the world will not be the same for years to come. This means that we should think about our own mortality and our own lives to find the best future we can for ourselves and our families.

As you will see later, this does not mean that we should become self-centred and selfish. On the contrary, the world needs kindness now more than ever.

We don't know yet what life will look like as things start to change, but surely this pandemic has already changed us in all kinds of ways we can't yet see. None of us really has the luxury of opting out, of just not thinking about it.

We may not be able to do much to change the world, but we can change our little corner of it.

Our journey is forward

We should abandon the question: When will we get back to normal? There will be no going back. The only way forward will be through. But the way through need not be bleak.

Our aim should be for a better life – and the pause forced on us by COVID-19 has given us a marvellous opportunity to find that way through.

This book, to be honest, will not solve all problems, heal trauma, or give a magical approach that will make it all better. But I hope it will give you a fresh way to look at your life and your family and how you can manage and make a better life.

We will get through this and one day we will have a story to tell of how we found our way through. It will be a story that will bring peace of mind to you and those you love.

Come. Let's see what the future could hold.

HOLD ON

A lesson
for all of us is
that for every loss,
there is victory,
for every sadness,
there is joy,
and when you think
you've lost everything,
there is hope.

Geraldine Solon

We are not all in the same boat

"Live the Life of Your Dreams: Be brave enough to live the life of your dreams according to your vision and purpose instead of the expectations and opinions of others."
Roy T. Bennett

"Walk with the dreamers, the believers, the courageous, the cheerful, the planners, the doers, the successful people with their heads in the clouds and their feet on the ground. Let their spirit ignite a fire within you to leave this world better than when you found it..."
Wilfred Peterson

"Courage is not having the strength to go on; it is going on when you don't have the strength."
Teddy Roosevelt

So here we are, struggling the best way we can to survive this Novel Corona Virus, COVID-19. Some of us have lost beloved family members or friends. Some of us have lost jobs. We've lost businesses, we've been isolated in our homes and forbidden to visit elderly relatives in nursing homes.

Politicians and others say we are all in the same boat, but it's not like that.

Not at all.

We are all facing life's journey and we do need each other, but, no, we're not all in the same boat. Your boat could be shipwrecked and mine might not be. Or vice versa. You might be rowing placidly on a calm lake. Your cousin might be caught in river rapids. Your neighbour might be adrift in a wild sea.

Look around you right now.

For some people, social distancing is relatively easy. For others, it's a devastating financial and family crisis. For some, it's depression and loneliness, while for others it's a time of relative peace and quiet family time.

Fortune did not favour all of us equally. That's not how life works. Some people received money from a government stimulus package, while others received not a penny.

Some have been ill with the virus, very ill, while others had no symptoms. Some are on their knees praying that a loved one will just get through the virus.

Others think it's nothing and don't believe a word they hear on television.

Some were stockpiling toilet paper and sanitizer and food they thought they might run short of one day. Others struggled to get to a supermarket, fearful that they would catch the virus, and then found nothing but empty shelves.

Some are bringing home more money than they were before the virus, while others are working longer hours for less money, and others are desperate to get back to work. Any work.

Some are spending long hours helping children with home schooling, while others do what they can, exhausted from working all day.

All of us were confused when some "experts" told us we were beating this curse of a virus, while others warned that the worst is yet to come.

Same boat?

I don't think so.

Where should life take us?

We are all rowing like mad and most of us will break out of the storm sooner or later. But every journey, *every journey*, is different.

My journey is not your journey. Yours is not mine. We each have to find our own way.

While COVID-19 is raging, we should all find what time we can to think about the future. Are we happy with our lives so far? Is there a better lifestyle we could aim for? Should our priorities in life change? Have the things that are truly important to us changed? Do we see things differently now?

Dare we hope for better?

The Covid-19 pandemic has disrupted our lives in ways we could not have imagined.

Who could have dreamed, as we approached Christmas 2019, that we would soon lose so many lives to a vicious, invisible disease? Suffer such anguish trying to pay bills and keep the roof over our head after losing work?

Who could have imagined we would be confined to our homes, isolated from friends and, sometimes, family?

And who would have thought it possible that loved ones, including the elderly and children, would have to fight for every desperate breath and finally die, alone with no family for support?

This pandemic has been cruel, heartless and unfair. Few have escaped its clutches and it has inflicted untold suffering on people who were already disadvantaged – the poor, the homeless, the sick, the refugees, the mentally ill, the lonely.

However, there are many good people on this planet. They might not have wings, but they are angels still, doing God's work. There were those preparing meals and finding toilet paper or sanitizer for elderly neighbours. There were children drawing rainbows and putting them in front windows to cheer passers-by.

Other children were writing letters to residents of nearby nursing homes, alone, isolated and not allowed visitors.

There were people making meals for nurses and doctors working long shifts.

When trouble comes, the world is full of heroes. And where would we be without them? But sometimes, we all have to do more than we think we can.

Tough times have to be overcome for the sake of each other and our families.

Our anxiety and fears are real and we have to face them. When the going gets tough, the tough get going. And we can all be tough when we need to be for our loved ones. We can't allow ourselves to be bogged down with misery. Let's leave the mire and aim for higher.

I think we should all listen to that still, small voice that tries to encourage us, rather than that loud, obnoxious one that screams about our inability to cope and to survive.

We must get over our obstacles and one way to do that is to stop aiming for perfection. Perfection is a myth.

What we should aim for is the best we can do in the time we have and whatever circumstances we face.

We can all do that.

Mark Twain was a funny man, but he worried just like the rest of us. "I've worried about a great many things in my life," he said. "Most of them never happened."

Let's set aside our fear that something might go wrong and start being excited about what could go right.

What should your life be like?

We all get to dream, don't we? What are your dreams? What do you value? What do you believe in? Why do you want to do with your life? These are questions for our quiet time, aren't they? Our solitude. We're not going to find answers to important questions in the chaos and noise of our everyday lives.

Many of us have the opportunity now, in our social isolation, to think about our life, what we like about it and what we do not like. How could life be better than it has been?

This is very personal, isn't it? One size will not fit all here.

There are suggestions in this book, but they are not, and cannot be, specific. All anyone can do for each of us is to perhaps give us a new way of looking at life. Then we can each set our imagination free.

So imagine it and dream it. If we can imagine it, and believe it's possible and that we deserve it, we can achieve it. No two ways about it.

When you find what is important to you - what you want in your life - you will have taken the first massive step to achieving that better life you want. Start the journey from pandemic to a better life by deciding what would be better *for you*.

Let solitude be your friend

Solitude: We are stuck with it as we try to contain the virus, and, for many of us, it's frustrating and depressing. But I believe it also gives us an opportunity we never anticipated to pause and think about our lives.

It gives us a chance to decide whether we want to get back to the old normal or whether we really want something new, something better.

More than three centuries ago, the French philosopher Blaise Pascal declared words that ring true today: "All of humanity's problems," he said, "stem from man's inability to sit quietly in a room alone."

Rev. Sunday Adelaja, pastor of a mega church in the Ukraine, says: "Without solitude, we are overwhelmed by all the things we hope to do and all of the things we are planning and praying to do, but we never really have the time to actually get down and get these things done."

That's the problem and solution in one sentence. Sure, our minds have been out of control much of the time and there were too many demands on our time. Our lives are so busy we can't draw breath to get on with what we want now, let alone in the future.

Answer? Solitude. Alone time. Silence. A chance for the hyperactive mind to slow down and think clearly and creatively.

A chance to order our life and put purpose into it.

In these rare periods of social isolation or quarantine, alone with our thoughts, we can see our lives from a different perspective and look at troubles differently. We can find the balance and confidence we need to face the world and our own future in it. Given enough time and space, we can find what is meaningful to us, what is important to us.

Solitude does take some getting used to, I'll grant you that. But it does grow on you and you grow in it.

"I live in that solitude which is painful in youth," said Albert Einstein, "but delicious in the years of maturity."

In times like these, I think the young need to run a bit faster to catch that maturity bus. We can't just sit around at the bus stop waiting.

One person who loves life is Mexican writer Akiroq Brost. This is what she said about quiet time: “Learn to be alone. Learn to love yourself,” she said. “Learn to spend time with yourself. Learn to cherish time with yourself. The cure for loneliness is solitude." Take some time to think about that.

Solitude cures loneliness.

Solitude is a great treasure and through it we can rebuild our lives, solve life's problems and create something new and exciting.

And it gives us time to work out how to be better ourselves. How to be more useful or effective or simply more loveable. How to discover the kind of person we want to be.

Good people needed

I firmly believe that good people are needed for a good, worthwhile world. A base of good values and principles in ourselves will give authenticity to everything we do. If we want to produce work that is useful and valued, we have to be useful and valued ourselves.

The best loved people are good people who try to offer service to others.

Sunday Adelaja is among many who urge solitude as the best place to think about our place in the world.

"Solitude helps you convert your time into clarity of purpose," he wrote. "You get a clearer picture of what your life should be like in the place of solitude... The power of imagination is strongest in that place...

"One of the greatest discoveries you could actually discover in life is the treasure of solitude."

Anne Frank treasured silence in her frightening, hidden world during World War II in The Netherlands. She wrote a beautiful little book, a journal of her life and times, and it's still read today.

"I can shake off everything as I write," she said. "My sorrows disappear, my courage is reborn." In a life of terrifying seclusion, silence and writing saved this young girl's sanity for a long time.

To understand the world in troubled times, sometimes it helps to turn away from it, according to one man who experienced more than most of us ever will and learned to love the solitude and silence of his ashram, Mahatma Gandhi.

This is where he learned to cope with the stresses he faced and the changes he had to make in his life to keep his quest for Indian independence alive. We have different needs now, after a pandemic, but quiet time gives us a chance to think.

The joy of helping others

When we are trying to think of what we can do to make our lives better, we can sometimes become overwhelmed by the choices we could make. The world (without COVID-19 anyway) is a big and wide wonderful world with opportunities everywhere we look, if we know where and how to look. The world is full of abundance, including an abundance of opportunity.

One simple piece of advice is still around after many years of being passed from one generation to another. It's still around because it's as perennial as the grass and as practical as the first time a wise old man wandered out of his cave and thought of it.

Find a need and fill it.

What could be simpler? It works at every level of your life and at whatever level of complexity you want to apply it. No matter what problem you are facing right now as you contemplate the future, this simple formula can surely help.

Think about your talents, your experience, your ability. Think about the things you like to do. How could you help people best? What do people need that you could do for them?

Whether you are thinking of a hobby or a career or just a change of pace or lifestyle, start with what you could do to make life better for others. Whatever would make life better for you could perhaps be the very thing to help others, and you could be the one to make things happen.

Looking for happiness? The one sure place to find it is in helping others.

My wife, Judy, and I have had a blessed life, but there were plenty of struggles as we faced tough times and uncertain futures. We each found our niche fairly late in life after year upon year of just doing our best, one foot in front of the other, trying to do what we had to do to keep house and home together and raise a family.

When it came right down to it, we both found joy and happiness doing what we could for others.

Judy still works in the next room to me as a mortgage broker because she loves helping people find a home, while I do what I can to help people with my quill. We both absorb ourselves in our work as much as we can in the circumstances we face. It takes our minds off ourselves, our problems and our worries and gives us breathing space. Judy's work and my writing are preserving our sanity in a world that sometimes seems to conspire against us.

On the journey, we both experienced sadness, disappointment, betrayal, heartbreak, pain and all the things we all face on our separate journeys. But, along the way, no matter what we faced, we searched for, and came away with, peace of mind and little pockets of serenity. What we also found was happiness.

I write, as I always have as a journalist, an editor and a publisher, to help people - to make their world a little bit better.

Here are some words I treasure on sorrow from a wonderful writer, Anna Lindsay, speaking about ploughing on regardless of how tough the ride:

The life that has not known and accepted sorrow is strangely crude and untaught. It can neither help nor teach, for it has never learned. The life that has spurned the lesson of sorrow, or failed to read it aright, is cold and hard, but the life that has been disciplined by sorrow is courageous, and full of holy and gentle love... Every tear that falls from one's own eyes gives a deeper tenderness of look, of touch, of word that shall sooth another's woe. Sorrow is not given to us alone that we may mourn. It is given us, that, having felt, suffered, wept, we may be able to understand, love, bless.

Life was never meant to be easy. That's why we should all try to find ways in which our experiences can help others – because, in doing so, we help ourselves.

Your hero might be you

There are many opportunities waiting for us when we seek a better life - we just have to be open to them. And we must take the plunge and do what we need to do to make life better for ourselves and our families.

They say God helps those who help themselves.

"I read and walked for miles at night along the beach," said poet Anna Quindlen, "writing bad blank verse and searching endlessly for someone wonderful who would step out of the darkness and change my life. It never crossed my mind that that person could be me."

There will always be a flower for those who look for one. Many of us want to be better and have a better life.

We just don't realize just how close that better life might be. The good life can be elusive, but, when we find it, we must make it ours.

I'm a writer, so I hope you don't mind if I use other writers to make my points.

English writer Neil Gaiman spoke of the uniqueness in each of us: "The one thing that you have that nobody else has is you," he said. "Your voice, your mind, your story, your vision. So, write and draw and build and play and dance and live as only you can."

That's it, isn't it? There is only one you. Make the most of what you find in you.

So, let's make a start

In weird, unpredictable times like these, it's easy to let old habits and even old traumas invade our thoughts and cause stress we don't need. It's stressful enough to find new ways to support our families, cope with illness, educate the kids (often from home), care for those who need us and cope with isolation.

If you were already struggling before the virus hit, life is even harder.

Yet, even in times of turmoil and disaster, there are small blessings to be found. If, during this crisis, we can think clearly and differently, there can be a light at the end of the tunnel.

Lots of people are making changes, big and small, in their lives to get through tough times. Many are starting to question the meaning of life if it can be snatched away so easily. They are thinking of what is worthwhile in life, what is important. What would make my life better?

This is an opportunity that we should not miss.

I'm very impressed with the young of this world these days, but let's hear from a young girl fearing for her life during World War II, Anne Frank: "How wonderful it is that nobody need wait a single moment before starting to improve the world."

How wonderful indeed. Most of us are concerned at the moment, but most of us do not fear for our lives. We just want to be safe and find a better life for ourselves and our loved ones.

When we face change in our lives, there are a few things worth remembering.

Life will only change when we start to focus on what we want, rather than what we had. We have to be willing to leave our comfort zone behind.

And, as Viktor Frankl said: "When we are no longer able to change a situation, we are challenged to change ourselves." Yes, it's hard to accept the fact that we sometimes need to change ourselves to achieve what we want.

Not everything we face in the world can be changed, but nothing will be changed until it is faced.

Don't let anyone tell you that what you want to do is impossible. How could anyone else possibly know what is impossible for you? I'd love a dollar for every time I did the impossible. There were always people willing to tell me what I could not do, but I did it anyway. I'm not smart – just willing to give it a go.

When I researched and wrote a major book, *The Life of Jude: Saint of the Impossible,* I had no idea that it was "impossible". It took me 50 years, but I did it anyway.

Pablo Picasso said: "I am always doing that which I cannot do, in order that I may learn how to do it."

So join the Impossible Club with Pablo and me. You might be surprised at the wonderful company you find there. People like you.

Now, let's look at different ways life could be better.

"When we least expect it,
life sets us a challenge
to test our courage and
willingness to change.
At such a moment, there
is no point in pretending
that nothing has happened or in
saying that we are not yet ready.
The challenge will not wait.
Life does not look back.
A week is more than enough
time for us to decide whether
or not to accept our destiny."

Paulo Coelho

How could life be better?

"Love the moment. Flowers grow out of dark moments. Therefore, each moment is vital. It affects the whole. Life is a succession of such moments and to live each is to succeed."
Corita Kent

"Don't allow your past or present condition to control you. It's just a process that you're going through to get you to the next level."
T.D. Jakes

"The biggest risk is not taking any risk… In a world that's changing really quickly, the only strategy that is guaranteed to fail is not taking risks."
Mark Zuckerberg

Everyone is on a journey and each of us have our own map. My map is of no use to you. Your map is of no use to me. And your map is none of my business, right? I'm going to assume that we could all do with improvements to our lifestyle, whether they be big changes or just tinkering around the edges.

We each have to dig deep to find our better life. No-one else can do it for us.

Argentine writer and poet, Jose Luis Borges, said it beautifully: "Plant your garden and decorate your own soul, instead of waiting for someone to bring you flowers."

So, let's talk about a better life and what it might mean. This might be a bit difficult for some. How do we work out how we would like our life to change? Well, I've got a crazy idea.

One way to work out what our life should be like is to think about the end of it – the eulogy. Yes, eulogy.

Why on earth would I want to talk about eulogies? Well, eulogies are the words spoken about us when we are stuck in a wooden box and can no longer speak for ourselves.

What words would we like to hear in our eulogy? What does it matter? Well, I'm sure we'd all like to think that some kind words could be found for us.

But what words? And why would this help us now? It's important now because we can influence what a friend would say about us by how we live. Now. And if we think now about what we'd like people to think of us, we will be guided by that to live well - and by well, I mean properly guided by a fine set of principles and values.

A eulogy is a peculiar thing. It pays little or no attention to what the world generally considers important. At our funerals, our friends will evaluate and celebrate our lives differently from the way the world views success in the living.

It pays to think of this now, because we can easily become so engrossed in and absorbed by our work that we neglect the things and the people that truly matter to us. It's easy to get so caught up in the busyness of living that we forget our values and forget the people we are living with. Our loved ones.

Your eulogy might well be the first time someone tries to evaluate our essence and our real worth to family, friends and society. It's how people remember us and what part of us is preserved in their hearts and minds.

So, how would you like to be remembered? What would make you feel good about yourself down the track a bit?

As you go through this book, why not start making notes about what changes you would like to see in your life? What would make others – family, friends, work colleagues – glad to be your friend?

Could a change in your approach to life trigger thoughts of appreciation and respect in your friends?

Please be patient and you will be rewarded. I know that, for many, life may not look so rosy just now, but I agree with actor Peter Sellers, who said this: "Let us learn to appreciate there will be times when the trees will be bare, and look forward to the time when we may pick the fruit."

One of my all-time favourite teachers and philosophers, William James, said: "The greatest discovery of my generation is that human beings can alter their life by altering their attitude."

Let me finish this thought of eulogies with the words of Joan Baez: "You don't get to choose how you will die. Or when. You can only decide how you are going to live. Now."

You are responsible for you

"The greatest lesson of life is that you are responsible for your life," said Oprah Winfrey.

The changes we choose for our lives need not be grand or complex.

When Mahatma Gandhi died, the world saw a photograph of all his earthly possessions: a pair of sandals, some clothes, a spinning wheel, his spectacles, a book. That was all.

And yet, was not Gandhi one of the most successful of men?

The writer who inspired me more than anyone else to want to be a writer, Robert Louis Stevenson, gave as good a description of success as I've ever seen:

"That person is a success who has lived well, laughed often and loved much; who has gained the respect of intelligent people and the love of children; who has filled a niche and accomplished the task at hand; who leaves the world better than he found it, whether by an improved poppy, a perfect poem or a rescued soul; who never lacked appreciation of earth's beauty or failed to express it; who looked for the best in others and gave the best he had."

I think all of those things Stevenson mentioned are very much achievable by both you and me.

We just need to use our imagination - and the imagination is a very potent weapon.

Imagine your goals

To use my imagination, I use a few imaginary tools and I'd like to tell you about one of them. It's all about setting goals.

My goals tool is an imaginary compass because the important thing to know is not so much where we are, but in which direction we are moving.

The Spanish/Roman philosopher, Seneca, said this: "When you don't know what harbour you are making for, no wind is the right wind."

Sometimes it's not possible to keep moving forward. Sometimes we have to take two steps back to regroup, reorganise, refresh - then we can move forward again.

Some people complain that life's an uphill battle. That's OK. At least you're heading in the right direction - you're climbing.

Make use of such an imaginary compass. It will be of no use to you if you don't have a goal, somewhere or something or someone you want to reach, but, once you have a goal, you have to stay on course to reach it.

I hope you pick a goal that's right for you and your family; that you choose to do the right thing always; choose to do what's right for those who come after you. I hope you find something that's a challenge, that's worthwhile, that will make the world just a little better for your passage through it.

With this imaginary compass, you won't find true north, but there's every chance you'll find your true self.

Imagination unlimited

"Your time is limited, don't waste it living someone else's life," said Steve Jobs. "Don't be trapped by dogma, which is living the result of other people's thinking. Don't let the noise of another's opinion drown your own inner voice. And most important, have the courage to follow your heart and intuition. They already know, somehow, what you truly want to become. Everything else is secondary." Follow your heart. It knows the way.

As an old coach of mine said: If you don't have a goal, you spend your life running up and down the field and never score.

Our own thoughts and imagination, or lack of them, are the only limits to our possibilities in life. Are you worried about risks ahead? The biggest risk is not taking any risk, according to the quote we just read from Mark Zuckerberg.

"In a world that's changing really quickly, the only strategy that is guaranteed to fail is not taking risks."

The biggest failure is way better than not trying. Even if you're going through hell, keep going. You can't stop there.

"It is not because things are difficult that we do not dare," said Seneca. "It is because we do not dare that things are difficult."

Few of us will be in the position of being able to change the world, but all of us can be able to change *our* world. To do that, we don't need possessions or power or position or prestige. We simply need what we find in ourselves - goodness, humility, service and character. That's what we need to change our world.

Let me tell you about something that changed my world and served me well for many years. It has given me a fresh sense of beauty, a sense of magic in the arts, and a feeling of serenity and peace I can call up whenever I need it. If I could bottle that sense of serenity, I reckon I could make my fortune.

I was only about 10 and staying with my aunt and uncle. I was mainly left to find my own amusement, but, one morning, Uncle Russ called me into his inner sanctum, a room I had never been in.

He put his finger to his lips to indicate silence and opened up a big, magical box.

It was made out of polished timber and I had never seen anything like it.

The Magical Box

From another cupboard, he took something black and round like a dinner plate. He put it in the magical box and the look in his eyes told me that something absolutely wonderful was about to happen.

It was.

From out of that magical box came the most unbelievably beautiful sounds I had ever heard. For an hour or more I was utterly transported, and so, I could tell, was my uncle.

This was my introduction to classical music and it was one of the most memorable lessons in my life. I have loved classical music ever since and it will always be part of me, a very special part.

Since that morning with Uncle Russ, my world has been more alive, more serene, more at ease, and more ready to wait and expect good things to happen.

Everything that makes us unique, makes us *us*, should be stored and used to make our lives better. That's how we quietly but surely make our lives better for us.

Use what talents and virtues and goodness you possess. The forests would be very quiet if no birds sang except those who sang well.

Do you deserve a better life?

Let's listen to Anne Frank again: "The good news is that you don't know how great you can be! How much you can love! What you can accomplish! And what your potential is!"

Ignore others when they say you are not worthy and not deserving of a better life. The only words you should focus on are those you speak to yourself. Your opinion is the only one that matters. Speak kindly to yourself. Believe.

William James was a keen observer of the human condition. "Believe that life is worth living," he said, "and your belief will help create the fact."

Poet Robert Frost said that he could sum up in three words everything he had learned about life: *It goes on*. Be part of it. Don't give up. Don't settle for any less than you deserve. We are all stronger than we know. Our strength comes from what we have been through, our struggles and hardship. It has all prepared us for today.

Remember: *Up to this point in your life, you have survived every single one of your worst days.*

So, dust off that imagination of yours. It grows more vivid and more ardent with use. Knowing how to use it will allow you to see beauty others miss, to solve problems that baffle others, to see beyond words and gestures into minds and hearts.

Use it to create, rather than destroy, to make things better than they were, to bring joy where there was pain, to bring comfort where there was grief.

The extent to which you use imagination will largely determine your power and capabilities in any situation and will determine whether you reach your potential.

Imagination will give you a sense of adventure and discovery that can reshape your world - and a sense of vision that can lead you to undreamed of success.

In the Louvre can be seen the magnificent painting of Goethe's Faust. It depicts Mephistopheles and Faust playing chess. Mephistopheles points and says, "Checkmate!", while Faust sits dejected. One day a master chess player was admiring the painting when he suddenly cried: "Satan, one minute! Faust has one more move!"

Imagination can usually help us find one more move. And that is often all we need.

The greatest book has not yet been written, the greatest song not yet sung, the greatest challenge not yet met, the greatest medicine not yet discovered, the greatest puzzles of life and death not yet solved. Your best life has yet to be created. The best is yet to be. Imagination and knowledge can make it so.

Why are you here?

Find your purpose, your reason for living. Answer the question: How can I serve others? I think I read every word the inspirational supremo, Og Mandino, ever wrote: "Always render more and better service than is expected of you," he said, "no matter what your task may be."

He echoed the words of my old high school science teacher, Brother Kerr. He was a giant of a man, a serious scientist, and he was very serious (and a little bit frightening) when he spoke to me one day. It was a long time ago, but I have never forgotten his words or his passion.

"Whatever you chose to do with your life, wherever your career path takes you, always strive to be the best you can be."

Always strive to be the best you can be. He didn't want me to compete with others - only with my own previous best. Dream your big dreams and be the best you can be.

Many years ago, when I was a boy, I was helping my father build our house. One particular day was cold and wet with persistent drizzling rain. I had visions of a warm room and a good book, but we worked on. I probably looked as miserable as the day, but I was very proud to be doing this work with dad.

He turned to me at one point and said something I've never forgotten: "We have to do the best we can, no matter what. And what we make has to be good. It has to last."

It has to be good. It has to last.

"A dream doesn't become reality through magic," said Colin Powell. "It takes sweat, determination and hard work."

But we're up for that, aren't we? So let's look at aspects of living that might help us find peace of mind and the life of our dreams.

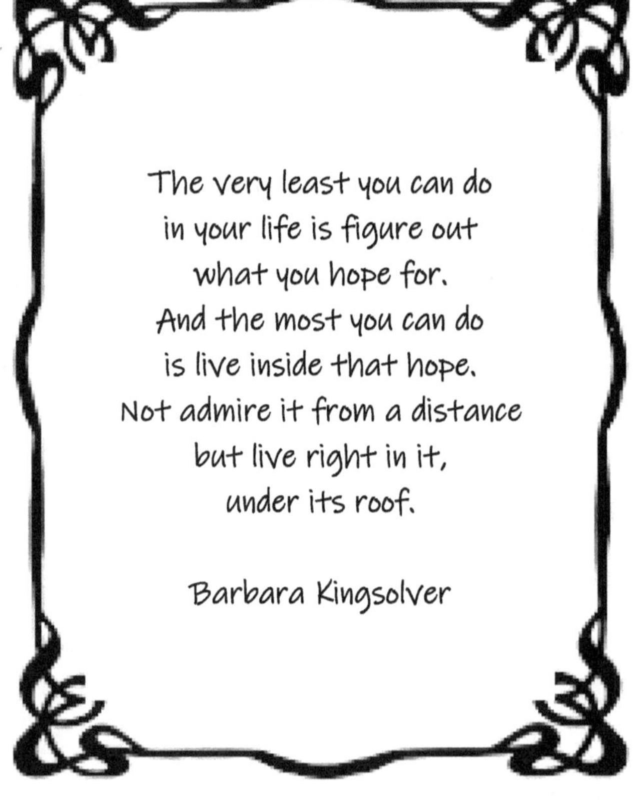

The very least you can do
in your life is figure out
what you hope for.
And the most you can do
is live inside that hope.
Not admire it from a distance
but live right in it,
under its roof.

Barbara Kingsolver

Simplify, Simplify

"Too many people spend money they haven't earned to buy things they don't want to impress people they don't like."
Will Rogers

"Besides the noble art of getting things done, there is the noble art of leaving things undone. The wisdom of life consists in the elimination of non-essentials."
Lin Yutang

"If you look at what you have in life, you'll always have more. If you look at what you don't have in life, you'll never have enough."
Oprah Winfrey

I think the first thing we should consider in post-virus life is simplicity. Just how chaotic or complex is your life? During the crisis, we were forced to return to the basics, weren't we? And, if we think about it, that return to the fundamentals had its advantages, did it not?

As the complexities of our lives dropped away, we found that we needed less to sustain our families and ourselves. It troubled us, at first, because we thought we needed to hold on to everything we had before the virus hit. But many of us started to realise that, by reducing confusion, life became beautifully simple again.

So, let's talk about simplicity and what it can do for us. But, before we do, we need to pause for a moment to consider the decisions and choices we'll face in our quest for a better life.

The gift of choice. I know you already have it because you couldn't live without it, but I want to make you more conscious of it.

This is the best and worst of gifts. Much of the stress of life would be gone if we didn't have to make decisions, but it wouldn't be much of a life, would it? We'd be no more than helpless babies, or plankton floating aimlessly in the sea.

Sometimes we wonder if we should change our lives. Well, we do change our lives - every day, countless times.

We change our lives when we choose one job over another, one house over another, one friend over another. We change our lives when we decide to have a baby, a pet, a hobby, a television, a computer - or none of them.

We change our lives when we put off a task or do it now, stay in bed or get up, rest or work, smile or frown, exercise or laze about, eat junk or fruit, play with the kids or ignore them.

We change our lives when we hurry or delay, worry or relax, plan or drift, love or hate, whistle or curse.

We change more than we realise.

Change your life? It's easier than you think. In fact, you do it all the time without thinking. Think how much better life could be if you did give choice a bit more thought.

Confucius said that life is really simple, but we insist on making it complicated. And he spoke those words before technology exploded and invaded every aspect of our lives.

He said it before the world lost its innocence and embraced complexity.

We once lived in a world of civility and peace and love. Modern civilisation is complicated and, in many ways, artificial.

Then we added hate and hate crimes and terrorism and we thought that was our permanent state – until COVID-19 changed everything.

Now we each have the chance to change the world – or at least our little corner of it. We can all change ourselves and create that better life for ourselves and our families.

The love of wisdom

As author E.A. Bucchianeri put it: "There are times when wisdom cannot be found in the chambers of parliament or the halls of academia but at the unpretentious setting of the kitchen table."

Our life is frittered away by detail, said Henry David Thoreau, of Walden fame.

"Simplify, simplify," he cried.

My grandfather started me on a lifelong love of wisdom.

"Any halfway intelligent fool can make things bigger or faster or more complex or even more violent," he said. "You're smarter than that. Make things better and simpler. That's the way to contentment."

Simplifying really comes down to prioritising, doesn't it? What is important? What is worthwhile? What can be dropped? Let's get rid of possessions or activities or even associations that are no longer necessary for our new life.

If things are no longer of value to us, they are simply clutter.

Sometimes old advice is still good advice. As ancient Chinese philosopher, Lao Tzu, put it: "Manifest plainness, embrace simplicity, reduce selfishness, have few desires."

We have to learn to let go. If we find ourselves clinging to our "stuff", we have to take charge of our lives and hack away at what is not essential.

"Simplicity is about subtracting the obvious and adding the meaningful," said writer John Maeda. Now there's a thought. If we add what is meaningful for our new lives, there simply will not be room for what is weighing us down.

What remains comes alive

"My task is to simplify and then go deeper, making a commitment to what remains," said author Sue Bender, in *Plain and Simple: A Journey to the Amish*. "That's what I've been after. To care and polish what remains till it glows and comes alive from loving care."

We don't need to become Amish, but we could borrow from their lifestyle as islands of sanity in a fast, complex world.

Albert Einstein believed that.

"Possessions, outward success, publicity, luxury - to me these have always been contemptible. I believe that a simple and unassuming manner of life is best for everyone, best for both the body and the mind."

Dolly Parton wrote about life in *Dolly: My Life and Other Unfinished Business.*

"They think I'm simple-minded because I seem to be happy," she wrote. "Why shouldn't I be happy? I have everything I ever wanted and more. Maybe I am simple-minded. Maybe that's the key: simple."

Our lives are unfinished business, are they not? I think we should aim for happy, too.

How do we do that?

Simple steps, one at a time. Remember what Lin Yutang said in *The Importance of Living*: "Besides the noble art of getting things done, there is the noble art of leaving things undone. The wisdom of life consists in the elimination of non-essentials."

The art of priorities

That wise old grandfather of mine used to say that the first step in making the kind of life you want is to dump everything you don't.

"A simple life is not seeing how little we can get by with - that's poverty - but how efficiently we can put first things first," said author Victoria Moran. "When you're clear about your purpose and your priorities, you can painlessly discard whatever does not support these, whether it's clutter in your cabinets or commitments on your calendar."

One of my wife's favourite writers is Sarah Breathnach, author of *Simple Abundance: A Daybook of Comfort and Joy*. She wrote: "Every day offers us simple gifts when we are willing to search our hearts for the place that's right for each of us."

Everything has to be right for us. The precious moments in life are often found in quiet moments with loved ones. We have to make room in our lives for such moments. Regardless of what work we face or what demands are being made on our time, my wife and I always start the day with a cup of tea together. Every day, for us, has to start in a serene and graceful way.

It's a little ritual. Could little rituals boost your joy of living and create wonderful memories for you? That's how life is truly lived, isn't it? Moments of simplicity and beauty.

"As you simplify your life, the laws of the universe will be simpler," said Henry David Thoreau. "Solitude will not be solitude, poverty will not be poverty, nor weakness weakness."

The simple life turns away from thoughts of what we do not have to thoughts of the things we do have. Gratitude is the attitude that fosters peace of mind.

Let me tell you a little story about how I learned, as a young boy, about giving and receiving, about sharing, about gratitude and about love. My Mum could not afford to buy two ice-cream cones, so she just bought one for me.

I'm sure Mum would have taught me this, but every time she bought me an ice-cream, I'd break off the little tip of the cone, scoop a little ice-cream in it and give it to her, so we both had an ice-cream. The look on her face and the sounds she made told me she loved her tiny cone just as much as I did my big cone.

So much to learn from such a simple little gesture.

Simplicity, love, gratitude. The raw ingredients of a beautiful life.

Two ways to be rich

As the inspirational author Alan Cohen said: "Simplicity is not the opposite of wealth. It is the door to the riches you already own."

There are two ways to be rich: You can acquire a great deal, or you can desire very little. Sometimes you already have more than you know. I wrote a book about that, called *You Are Already Rich.*

Maybe you don't need to work like crazy to enjoy wonderful holidays.

Perhaps you could live the kind of life that made you happy every day.

The journey towards simplicity can be an emotional one. As you dig deeper into your life, you find that strong currents run deep. Here's what author Lisa J. Shultz wrote in *Lighter Living: Declutter, Organize, Simplify*:

"In the process of decluttering things in my life, I was peeling off the layers of my past that no longer mattered to my present life. But as I did that shedding, memories and emotions arose. I sometimes felt sadness as I removed reminders of a failed marriage or the loss of a loved one. I grieved lost dreams and deceased people and pets. If I looked for it, I also experienced gratitude for the good times and the love that once was. Eventually, I felt lighter after I worked my way through a particular emotional zone that exposed remnants of unhealed parts of my life."

Take that emotional journey. Now is the time. Take the time to observe the simple things that give you joy and the things that, though insignificant, mean a great deal to you and your family.

Life can be beautiful.

Someone once said that simplicity and elegance are sometimes indistinguishable. The best things in life cannot be seen with the eyes, they must be seen with the heart.

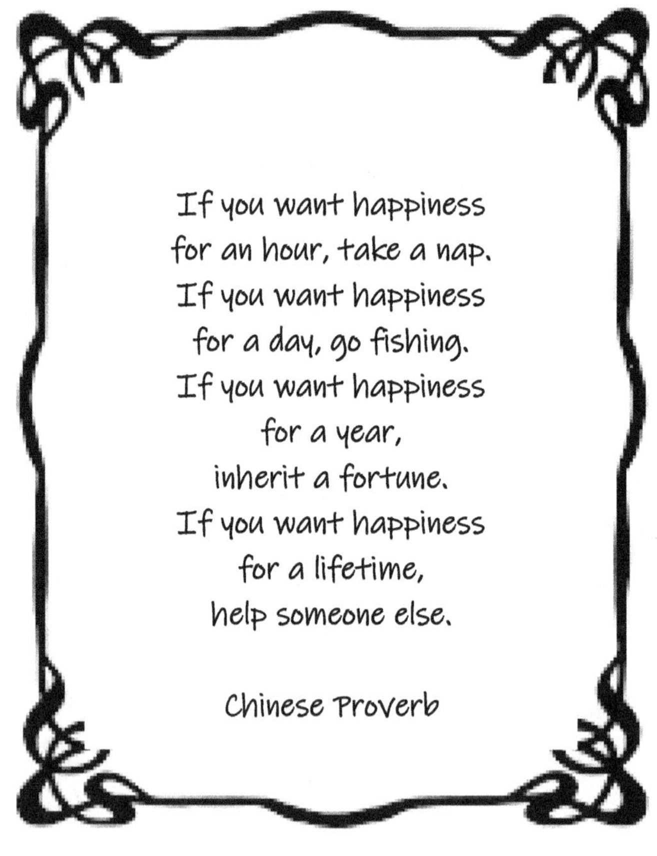

If you want happiness
for an hour, take a nap.
If you want happiness
for a day, go fishing.
If you want happiness
for a year,
inherit a fortune.
If you want happiness
for a lifetime,
help someone else.

Chinese Proverb

Finding the happiness we all deserve

"It isn't what you have or who you are or where you are or what you are doing that makes you happy or unhappy. It is what you think about it."
Dale Carnegie

"It is not how much we have,
but how much we enjoy,
that makes happiness."
Charles Spurgeon

"We tend to forget that happiness doesn't come as a result of getting something we don't have, but rather of recognizing and appreciating what we do have."
Frederick Keonig

When we come out of something as restrictive and limiting as the pandemic, the natural reaction is to seize moments of joy wherever we can with family and friends. Then life begins to settle into some kind of "new normal" in which we try to restore comforts and pleasures while we try to earn a meaningful living.

Beyond that, we should start to look for something better, should we not? The "old normal" left a lot to be desired, if we want to be honest. Now, surely, we deserve a chance at happiness.

That's not so easy when we're coming out of a fierce storm.

Adversity, if it brings nothing else, brings time for sober reflection. I wouldn't want to trivialise a pandemic, but a little rain clears the air and creates growth. Come to think about it, we couldn't live without rain. And I don't think we can hope for a better life if we don't pause to reflect on tough times and what we expect afterwards.

I'm reminded of a story told to me by the prolific author, Rabbi Brasch.

I was interviewing him on the occasion of his 80th birthday. We were in his living room, filled with mementoes of his travels and writing, and with magnificent views over Sydney Harbour.

I don't remember how his thoughts turned to worms, but they did.

It seems that a man discovered large earthworms in his garden and, curiosity aroused, he decided to experiment. He placed some worms on a smooth surface and some on rough ground. Before long, something interesting happened. The worms on the smooth surface became lethargic. Apparently they found life too monotonous and lost all their energy. The other group, by contrast, had to work hard on the rough terrain and began to thrive.

"Our road leads uphill all the way," Rabbi Brasch said. "Without a challenge, we become dull and listless. But adversity forces us to exert ourselves and is thus a stimulus to success."

So take the rough and hard luck when it comes and put the experience to work for you. Even a bird knows to sing after a storm, and I'm sure it's not just because it found the worms.

Let tears water seeds of joy

Setbacks, hardship, betrayal, sorrow - such things come to us all, but what we do with them is up to us. We can use the experience for ourselves and for others.

"Look," said Hans Christian Anderson, "contemplate the pearl of sorrow, for it contains the wings of the spirit, which carry us away from here."

May I repeat what Anna Lindsay said?

"The life that has not known and accepted sorrow is strangely crude and untaught. It can neither help nor teach, for it has never learned. The life that has spurned the lesson of sorrow, or failed to read it aright, is cold and hard; but the life that has been disciplined by sorrow is courageous, and full of holy and gentle love... Every tear that falls from one's own eyes gives a deeper tenderness of look, of touch, of word, that shall sooth another's woe. Sorrow is not given to us alone that we may mourn. It is given us, so that, having felt, suffered, wept, we may be able to understand, love, bless."

So cry if you have to, comfort those you love and learn the lessons. Your tears will water the seeds of your future happiness.

The As-if Principle

Life is difficult. Sometimes it's hard to feel happy, so you will need the As-If Principle, which was given to me by my favourite philosopher, William James, and which has served me well on the occasions I remembered to use it. It's yours now.

The principle is: If you want something, act as if you already had it.

OK, so you want to be happy? Act as if you are already happy. I think you'll discover, as I did, something special: If you smile a genuine smile, it is impossible to feel sad at the same time. Impossible.

Try it. Try it again. Keep on trying. Act as if...

Someone very close to me suffered trauma in his life and had a great deal of anger bottled up inside. He was young and had suffered much. I remember asking him to stand in front of the mirror and to retain his anger, while, at the same time, try to smile a genuine smile. The look on his face as he tried it was priceless, but he just could not manage it.

Whatever is most dominant in your thinking, happens. When you act as if you are happy, and persist, you become so. Really.

Happiness is so close; I hope you reach for it. It will keep you young, no matter what your age.

Peace of Mind

Someone said God gave us memory so that we might have roses out of season. I think he also gave it to bring us peace of mind. And peace of mind is a prerequisite for happiness, is it not?

You'll have memories of good times past and memories of lessons learned in isolation and social distancing. Sift through these memories on rainy days or sleepless nights. They will help while you plan the next phase of your life.

You have the capacity to store and treasure memories - limitless memories of things seen and felt and done, from which you can select an endless supply of nutrients to sustain your spirits.

Peace of mind will truly nurture you through rough seas and beyond.

Money, even a windfall, is no guarantee of happiness. Studies of lottery winners found they were no happier than people who hadn't won.

On the other hand, perhaps happiness can be a measure of how wealthy you really are. The Buddhist philosopher Nagajuna considered contentment to be the greatest form of wealth.

The best things in life, says the old song, are free.

Some say that success is getting what you want, while happiness is wanting what you get. This book talks about what is real in life, so let's go with the idea that happiness, when we find it, will be a real asset for us.

My grandfather grew prize-winning double dahlias and I have wonderful memories of an upright, happy man, very tolerant of a small boy running wild through his dahlia beds.

I'm at my happiest when I have a pen in my hand. In fact, I often say, and mean it, that I don't know what I think until I see what comes out of the end of my pen. On the other hand, my wife, Judy, is happy as a pig in mud when she's in her garden. She's a whiz in the garden, whereas I'm lethal. To each his own. We all have to seek our own joy in life.

Perhaps, as always, we should listen to old Abe Lincoln: "Most people are just about as happy as they make up their minds to be."

Spread joy wherever you find it

And here is another thing to remember about happiness. Mark Twain put it this way: "Grief can take care of itself, but to get the full value from happiness, you must have someone to share it with."

George Bernard Shaw agreed, but went further: "We have no more right to consume happiness without producing it than to consume wealth without producing it."

Here is an absolute truth: *Our most valuable possessions are those which can be shared without lessening; those which, when shared, multiply.*

Intangible gifts are the best gifts.

Happiness - the elixir of youth - is just one such thing.

I know that most of the time you won't need very much to keep you sane and in good spirits. That's why I want you to find something special in your life - a big bag of little bits.

A little bit of goodness, a little bit of courage, a little bit of grace, a small kindly thought. Look for a little bit of strength, a little bit of virtue, a little bit of truth (though a whole bit). A little bit of hope, a little bit of faith, a little bit of love.

It's up to you to find these "little bits" and put them to good use.

I'm sorry, but some of these little bits are a bit hard to control - they become big bits as soon as you begin to use them.

A little bit of the right attitude also helps. My wife and I have a very dear friend who has always had a positive, happy attitude to life. No matter how often you ask her: "How are you today, Rose?", her answer will always be the same: "Top of the world!"

It works for her.

At the time of writing, our friend is 105 years young and still a blessing to the world. We salute you, Mum Rose, and the joy you have always spread.

Peace of a different kind

British author and playwright Joyce Rachelle knows what is important in life. "If we can't have world peace, I'll settle for a quiet room." Oh yes, because what comes out of that quiet room is peace of a different kind - peace of mind.

The world is full of people searching for some kind of spectacular happiness. They are so busy looking, they miss the contentment all around them. I'm a writer, so I love a quiet room, but we all have our own idea of what happiness is for us.

When we do find it, we'll often realise it crept up on us while we were looking for something else.

Some say that achievement is the key to happiness, but that seems to me to be back-to-front.

And a certain explorer/philosopher/theologian you know agrees.

"Success is not the key to happiness," said Albert Schweitzer. "Happiness is the key to success. If you love what you are doing, you will be successful."

So, what is happiness?

Is there a way to work out the essential ingredients for happiness? Well, American author Dennis Lehane offers a few clues:

"Happiness doesn't lie in conspicuous consumption and the relentless amassing of useless crap. Happiness lies in the person sitting beside you and your ability to talk to them. Happiness is clear-headed human interaction and empathy. Happiness is home. And home is not a house - home is a mythological concept. It is a state of mind. A place of communion and unconditional love. It is where, when you cross its threshold, you finally feel at peace."

Sometimes we don't even realise we're happy, but, when we do, we find we have plenty to smile about.

Of course, you can find yourself smiling in all kinds of situations, as I have, some of them probably inappropriate. You've no doubt sometimes used a smile to mask disappointment and pain. It does the job very well, though close friends can see through it. But a true smile comes mainly unbidden. It's just there, delighting in beauty or love or success or fun or anything that tickles the fancy.

Smiles have value if given away

A smile costs nothing and takes up no time - you can do other things while you smile. No-one is so rich that a smile is not essential to enjoy it all. No-one is so poor that a smile won't enrich the day.

A smile is of no value unless it is freely given away, but, when given from the heart, it is priceless.

Some people are too busy to smile. Some are too sad. When you meet such people, give them a smile - they need it more than you know.

And be sure you don't become smile-deprived yourself. Don't be like the Caliph of Cordova, Abd-er-Rahman, who, about a thousand years ago, wrote: "I have now reigned more than fifty years in victory or peace, beloved by my subjects, dreaded by my enemies, and respected by my allies. Riches and honours, power and pleasure, have waited on my call. And no earthly blessing has been lacking in my life. In this situation, I have diligently numbered the days of pure and genuine happiness which have fallen to my lot. They amount to fourteen."

Oh dear.

Was Alexander the Great ever happy? He died at thirty-three, unhappy because he had no more worlds to conquer. What a shame. If only he had known what we know - that you don't have to conquer the world to claim its wonders for your own.

Now that's worth smiling about.

I want you to enjoy piles and piles of laughter - laughter of all kinds. No laughs at other people's expense, of course, but quiet chuckles, rib-tickling laughs, great belly laughs, tickle-your-fancy laughs, deep-down-inside laughs, infectious laughs, happy-to-be alive laughs, just-for-the-heck-of-it laughs, great bursts of laughter.

Nothing is quite as simple as laughter. The years have rolled on for me, but simple things stick in my memory. I remember a time, on a family picnic, my daughter began to tickle her toddler son. Before long, she didn't have to tickle, just look as if she was about to, and he'd burst into laughter. He laughed until he gasped for breath and I did, too. Soon we were all rolling around with laughter and aching with the exertion of it. All cares, worries and tensions were instantly banished.

Laughter is not harmless; it's deadly to stress.

Thackeray said laughter is sunshine in a house. I know for a fact it cures many ills; in fact, he who laughs, lasts.

And the best laughter is shared laughter. Share yours. Laughing is as contagious as a virus.

Where can we find happiness?

Happiness is often a by-product. We might be doing something else or mending a child's toy or trying to make someone else happy and suddenly serendipity hits us.

We realise that, somehow, happiness has crept up on us and surprised us.

Happiness, and where it comes from, is often a bit of a mystery.

"Everyone wants to live on top of the mountain, but all the happiness and growth occurs while you're climbing it," said Andy Rooney.

Ah, I think Frederick Koenig has hit the nail on the head: "We tend to forget," he said, "that happiness doesn't come as a result of getting something we don't have, but rather of recognizing and appreciating what we do have."

Something special happens when we look for happiness and try to spread it wherever we can. Inspirational author Shannon L. Alder got it right:

"When you are joyful, when you say yes to life and enjoy yourself and project positivity everywhere, you can become a sun in the centre of every constellation, and people want to be near you."

What a bonus when all you are trying to do is to make things a little bit better for yourself and your family. Happiness attracts friends.

I've heard it said that there are three things necessary for happiness in this life: Something to do, something to love, and something to hope for. The first two of these we've talked about: Having a purpose in life and having someone or something to love. But hope is something we rarely think about.

Hope. My wife and I cared for my mother through her dementia – and what a dreadful infliction that is. While caring for Mum, we came to realise that the really horrible thing about dementia is that sufferers, because they have lost their memory, have also lost all hope. Devastating.

So, in our journey from pandemic to a better life, we must, *must,* keep hope in our hearts and minds. Without it, we will get nowhere. We must remain positive and look for the best in whatever life throws at us.

It might be hard, but we can do it. Hold on to hope and hold on to happiness. My wife and I have had plenty of ups and downs in a long marriage, but we always believed we would get through whatever obstacle stood in front of us. Troubles? I'd love a dollar for every time we laughed at them.

I think I read everything Earl Nightingale ever wrote and he was a pretty smart man: "Learn to enjoy every minute of your life," he said. "Be happy now. Don't wait for something outside of yourself to make you happy in the future. Think how really precious is the time you have to spend, whether it's at work or with your family. Every minute should be enjoyed and savoured."

Yes, it should. Time is precious. Work at your plans, enjoy every minute of the journey, laugh at your small troubles and work around the big ones. Love what you do and those around you. Hang on to hope and happiness when you find them.

This is your life. Do you remember that I spoke of my 105-year-old friend, Rose? Rose has always had a saying: *Know what you want, believe you deserve it, and go for it!*

So, go for it. Make your life what you want it to be.

We can't be afraid of change.
You may feel very secure
in the pond that you are in,
but if you never venture
out of it, you will never know
that there is such a thing
as an ocean, a sea.
Holding onto something
that is good for you now,
may be the very reason
why you don't have
something better.

C. JoyBell C.

Real value, real worth

"Values are like fingerprints. Nobody's are the same but you leave them all over everything you do."
Elvis Presley

"I stand for honesty, equality, kindness, compassion, treating people the way you want to be treated, and helping those in need. To me those are traditional values."
Ellen Degeneres

"I have learned that as long as I hold fast to my beliefs and values, and follow my own moral compass, then the only expectations I need to live up to are my own."
Michelle Obama

Many of us focus on money and wealth. People can become obsessed with materialistic possessions, and no doubt many will remain that way as life returns to "normal". But many have never been like that and some who have been are now reassessing their priorities in life.

Perhaps there is a better way of living – less stressful, more meaningful.

That's the track we're walking in this book, the track to a better life. On this track, we're starting to think that changes should be made in our lives and that the only change we can be sure of is the change we decide to make in ourselves.

We've now come to a little clearing in the forest where we can quietly think of personal values. What is it that we could adopt in our character that would give us strength to face an uncertain future? What could give us self-assurance and confidence that our decisions along the way will be the right ones?

To find answers, we have to work out what is important to us, what is worthwhile in our lives. We have to think about what we believe in, what would be good for us and our families. And that kind of soul-searching leads us to our values – the characteristics that make us who we are and give us the base for the good life we desire.

Let's look for ideas that will help us on this quest. Let's see what writers and thinkers have said about this.

And, in this chapter, we'll find the simple rule that makes sense of everything and makes everything easy.

Words attributed to Albert Einstein are worth pondering: "Don't try to be a successful person, try to be a person of value. The successful person takes more out of life than he puts into it. The person of value gives more to life than he takes out of it."

This gives us our goal, which requires high ideals to reach. We all need ideals. I see no sense in having plenty to live on and nothing to live for.

First, you need a little courage

The first value we'll need as we change is courage.

I particularly want you to realise you have courage for when you need it. Not ordinary courage, the kind you need just to get by in life. You need the premium grade - the kind that kicks in when ordinary courage peters out. You know, when everything's against you and you can't hold on a moment longer.

The kind many of us had to find one way or another during the pandemic.

Do the impossible. Hang on. You can give up at any time - why do it now? The tide doesn't turn until its lowest ebb.

Hang on when you have nothing to hang on with, except courage premium grade.

Admiral Chester Nimitz is credited with this version of the famous prayer about courage:

"God grant me the courage to change the things
I can change,
the serenity to accept those I cannot change,
and the wisdom to know the difference –
but God grant me the courage not to give up
on what I think is right,
even though I think it's hopeless."

That last thought is sometimes missed, and sometimes we have to hang on until we understand what is right.

There are so many stories about courage. Poet William Ernest Henley wrote *Invictus,* containing the immortal words:

In the full clutch of circumstance
I have not winced nor cried aloud.
Under the bludgeoning of chance
My head is bloody but unbowed.

I have read the letter he wrote that told of the circumstances in which he penned that poem: "I was a patient," he wrote, "in the old infirmary of Edinburgh. I had heard vaguely of Lister, and went there as a sort of forlorn hope on the chance of saving my foot. The great surgeon received me, as he did and does everybody, with the greatest kindness, and, for twenty months, I lay on one or other ward of the old place under his care. It was a desperate business, but he saved my foot, and here I am."

During that "desperate business", Henley was writing some of the most inspired lyrics ever written about courage.

Henley's letter was addressed to Scottish rector, J.M. Barrie, who also received a letter from Captain Robert Falcon Scott of the Antarctic. You might remember Captain Scott and four of his party perished on an ill-fated expedition.

Here is how Rector Barrie spoke of Scott's letter:

An unforgettable letter

"It was found in his tent with his body and those of some other very gallant gentlemen, his comrades. The writing is in pencil, still quite clear, though towards the end some of the words trail away, as into the great silence that was waiting for them. It begins:

'We are pegging out in a very comfortless spot. Hoping this letter may be found and sent to you.

'I write you a word of farewell. I want you to think well of me and my end...

'Goodbye. I am not at all afraid of the end, but sad to miss many a simple pleasure which I had planned for the future ...

'We are in a desperate state - feet frozen, etc., no fuel, and a long way from food, but it would do your heart good to be in our tent, to hear our songs and our cheery conversation ...

'We are very near the end ... We did intend to finish ourselves when things proved like this, but we have decided to die naturally without.'."

Things are not so desperate for us, but I think it would do any heart good to stand beside that tent sometimes and listen to those "songs and cheery conversation."

Finding our value system

With courage, the quest for our own values system can begin. A values system will guide us when we are lost, as many of us will be at some stage of the journey.

According to author Hyrum W. Smith: "Your governing values should be important enough to you that you will invest your time, resources, and energy in making them a fundamental part of your life."

So, what are these values and principles we could use and adopt as our own? There are many and the list you make for yourself will be the best list for you.

You will, of course, have a set of values now, but you could consider honing up honesty and integrity, good manners, respect for others, patience, common sense, dignity, a sense of humour, morals, compassion, empathy, a willingness to work, serenity, gratitude. The list is endless and some values and principles will resonate more than others with you.

Money can't buy these things, can it? Each of these values, incorporated into our personalities and our character are simply priceless. Every person of goodwill loves and respects these things and will love and respect you when you adopt them and practise them in daily living and interacting with others.

One of the things I did not like about the pre-pandemic world was that too many people valued others by the size of their wallet or the brand of their car or the prestige of their house. As we found out during this pandemic and as we found during wars or wildfires or flood or cyclone – or even simply loss of a job – money, car and status can disappear much faster than it took to acquire them.

No. This is just "stuff" and should not be our primary concern.

If we can make ourselves as good as we can, according to our own principles and beliefs, then we will be able to attract possessions, but we are more important than the possessions around us. Of course, when a pandemic threatens to wipe out our possessions and we pause to consider what is really important for us, we begin to rethink what we do need in our lives. Our list of needs changes, doesn't it?

As author Jorge Amado put it: "A person's value does not rest on outward appearances, but on his true merits, what he really is."

Stephen Covey is another who believes that an authentic life of integrity is the most fundamental source of personal wealth.

"Peace of mind comes when your life is in harmony with true principles and values and in no other way," he says. "Moral authority comes from following universal and timeless principles like honesty, integrity, treating people with respect."

All kinds of people in all walks of life believe in what is authentic.

Zig Ziglar writes about personal success: "The foundation stones for a balanced success are honesty, character, integrity, faith, love and loyalty."

With strong values in your backpack, you will have something to live by and the arsenal to stand up for what you believe.

Add a little extra to ordinary

Old Abe Lincoln was a simple man and a kind one, and love for him in America has endured for many years. "When I do good, I feel good," he said. "When I do bad, I feel bad. That's my religion."

All parts of the world have their tragedies. In Australia, we have floods, drought, cyclones and bushfires. We also go to war too often. When each of these tragedies strike, I see ordinary people doing unbelievably extraordinary things. I've seen feats of heroism that are simply stunning. I live in absolute awe of my fellow human beings when trouble strikes.

However, I always remember what Ralph Waldo Emerson said: "Heroes are no braver than ordinary people, but they are brave five minutes longer."

Afraid? Don't worry. Fear has one master - courage - and courage has one weapon - action. For bravery to exist, there must first be fear, but action kills fear and brings bravery to life. I've seen it, and I think you have, too.

Heroism is based on a big heart and a solid foundation of good values: Compassion, courage, willingness to help, resilience, inner strength. These are nutrients for the soul.

There are values in all of us waiting to be put to good use. Things like harmony, integrity, honour, friendship, hopes and dreams, wisdom and the knowledge of right and wrong. These are the ingredients that make life magical and beautiful.

So many wondrous things to be seen if you look for them. Look for something beautiful every day and, when you find it, it is yours to carry you through many an obstacle.

You'd think a man of war would be too tough to think much of things like beauty, but listen to what General Douglas Macarthur had to say:

"In the central place of every heart there is a recording chamber; so long as it receives messages of beauty, hope, cheer and courage, so long are you young. When the wires are all down and your heart is covered with the snows of pessimism and the ice of cynicism, then only are you grown old."

I think he's right.

Morris Mandel tells of an unknown poet who described what he believed were four beautiful things:

These things are beautiful beyond belief:
The pleasant weakness that comes after pain,
The radiant greenness that comes after rain,
The deepened faith that follows after grief,
And the awakening to love again.

I think you and I can add to that list, don't you?

Blindness did not affect the vision of Helen Keller, author of *The World I Live In*.

"I have walked with people whose eyes are full of light, but who see nothing in woods, sea or sky, nothing in the city street, nothing in books. What a witless masquerade is this seeing. It were better far to sail forever in the night of blindness with sense and feeling and mind than to be thus content with the mere act of seeing. They have the sunset, the morning skies, the colour of distant hills, yet their souls voyage through this enchanted world with nothing but a barren stare."

Keller gave some advice to those who have the benefit of sight: Use your eyes as if tomorrow you would be struck blind. I think that our lives would be truly enriched if we tried to see everything as if it was the first time we could see it, or the last.

The world has so many riches we take for granted, but never take to our hearts.

The family must come first

Speaking of riches, I'd like to mention something close to my heart and, I think, very important to all of us.

We must put family first.

The notion that we have to shunt everything and everyone aside to create our masterpiece or our career is absolute nonsense. If we don't put family and friends first, how can we ever be anything but lonely? If we put family first and blend our work and our life with family, people will resonate with what we are doing and how we are living. People will love us for who we are.

Let this be the basis for the good life we seek.

So what, exactly, is the good life? We each must define what would be a good life for us. A group consensus is of no value here. We each must have our own clear destination so that we can trim our sails accordingly to get there.

The things our friends look for in us are our principles, our values, the things we believe in. They look for what our families mean to us, how we care, what we give, what we do for others. They love to see kindness and how we laughed together and what we went through together.

Real stuff. Things that matter. Love, honesty, courage, truth, morals. People we love. Things of value.

And let's include a sense of humour. "Always do what is right," said Mark Twain. "It will gratify half of mankind and drive the other half mad."

Love in action

My wife and I have been together 60 years. How? Well, we share similar values and principles, and we are there for each other. It's simply love in action. And, of course, she has infinite patience.

Oh, and we are a bit weird at times. When trouble comes, we face it, do what we have to do, then laugh at the trouble. We take life seriously up to a point, then fall back on our sense of humour. I have to say that, the older we get, the easier it becomes to laugh with each other and, in our "senior moments", laugh *at* each other.

"I love those who can smile in trouble, who can gather strength from distress, and grow brave by reflection," said Leonardo da Vinci. "Tis the business of little minds to shrink, but they whose heart is firm, and whose conscience approves their conduct, will pursue their principles unto death."

My wife and I try to live in such a way that, when our children and grandchildren think of caring and fairness and integrity and willingness to do our best, they might think of us.

I hope you might find the love and joy we found.

I wish you dreams because dreams let us see what might be and, having shown what might be, they put a breeze under our wings to lift us. Dreams bring wondrous things within reach.

Dreams are the promise of what will one day be.

Oh, and I promised you a simple rule to make all of this easy.

Becoming better with integrity simply comes down to practising the Golden Rule: *Treat others as you would like to be treated.*

We can all do that - and we have an opportunity now to reboot our good intentions.

FAMILY

Listen to the people
who love you.
Believe that they are worth
living for, even
when you don't believe it.
Be brave; be strong.
Exercise because it's good
for you, even if every step
weighs a thousand pounds.
Reason with yourself when you
have lost your reason.

Andrew Solomon

Let kindness be the next pandemic

Life is mostly froth and bubble,
Two things stand like stone.
Kindness in another's trouble,
Courage in your own.
Adam Lindsay Gordon

The smallest act of kindness is worth more than the greatest intention.
Kahlil Gibran

Beginning today, treat everyone you meet as if they were going to be dead by midnight. Extend to them all the care, kindness and understanding you can muster, and do it with no thought of any reward. Your life will never be the same again.
Og Mandino

In the old world order, many of us thought too much of "me" and not enough of "we". We forgot how much we needed each other and how, in earlier times, kindness had been the glue that kept us together.

It took an awful pandemic to remind us, I hope, of our shared vulnerability and to restore our collective humanity.

If you take the word "illness" and substitute "we" for "i", illness becomes wellness.

Of all the qualities that define us as human beings (and we mention many of them in this book) kindness must surely head the list.

Those who know me know that one of my favourite poets and thinkers is Lebanese American Kahlil Gibran, who said: "Tenderness and kindness are not signs of weakness and despair, but manifestations of strength and resolution."

I can't think, right now, of anything more important in life than an attitude of kindness.

"Three things in human life are important," said Henry James. "The first is to be kind; the second is to be kind; and the third is to be kind."

You don't necessarily have to be kind because someone else deserves it. Do it because you're a nice person.

"Attitude is a choice," said author Roy T. Bennett. "Happiness is a choice. Optimism is a choice. Kindness is a choice. Giving is a choice. Respect is a choice. Whatever choice you make makes you. Choose wisely."

A simple act of kindness, no matter how small, can make a mighty difference to the person who received it. Lives can change.

The thoughts of Chinese philosopher Lao-Tzu ring true today, perhaps even more so in these troubled times: "Kindness in words creates confidence. Kindness in thinking creates profoundness. Kindness in giving creates love."

You already have a wonderful attitude to giving, otherwise you would not be here seeking a better life for yourself and your family.

All of us receive, even in this imperfect world, more than we could possibly repay. Ordinary people are everyday heroes, as we have seen during the pandemic. As I was writing this, I had a call from a dear friend, who is by no means ordinary, but is certainly a pandemic hero.

This lady has been working with her church group to phone other parishioners every week to check if they are OK during isolation. If they need anything the group swings into action. When people are doing it tough, bags of groceries appear on their doorstep. I would never have known my friend was a hero because she is a retired doctor and doesn't talk about herself or the good that she does.

It just slipped out in our chat about the pandemic.

Our natural instinct is to do what is right, what is needed, for others. We are all blessed with abundance of one kind or another and we want to share it.

The gift of your own time

Albert Einstein said: "A hundred times every day I remind myself that my inner and outer life depend on the labours of other people, living and dead, and that I must exert myself in order to give in the same manner as I have received and am still receiving."

Albert Einstein gave plenty.

So did Plato, when he used his mind to grasp that beauty, truth and goodness were essential to the human race. Albrecht Durer gave the world his *Praying Hands*.

Handel had a paralysed limb, was destitute and facing imprisonment, but he gathered up his courage and wrote his greatest work, *The Messiah*.

Gifts often flow from suffering. French artist Pierre Auguste Renoir suffered greatly from rheumatism. It was extremely painful for him to paint, but he sat on a chair and kept at it.

A visiting friend saw his pain and asked: "Why do you continue to torture yourself?" Renoir thought for a while and replied: "The pain passes, but the beauty remains."

Renoir gave plenty.

Robert Louis Stevenson, who gave me so much pleasure in my younger years and inspired my urge to write, wrote to a friend in 1893 that he had not had one day of good health in fourteen years. Stevenson inspires me still. If he can do it, I can. And so, I believe, can you.

"I have wakened sick and gone to bed weary," he said, "and yet I have done my work unflinchingly. I have written my books in bed and out of bed, written them when my head swam with weakness... The battle still goes on - ill or well is a trifle so long as it goes."

Stephenson gave plenty.

So did others, despite obstacles. Beethoven was deaf, as was Milton. Homer was blind. Rembrandt was troubled, Alexander Pope a hunchback, Edgar Allen Poe a psycho-neurotic. Charles Darwin was an invalid, Julius Cesar an epileptic, Franklin D. Roosevelt a polio victim.

Perhaps our problems are not so great?

Those we touch on the journey

If we think about it, we don't want our lives to be defined by what is etched on our tombstones, do we?

I think we'd rather be remembered for what is etched in the hearts and lives of those we've touched on our journey.

Let our every deed and every word be etched with kindness.

"Don't let a cruel word escape your mouth," said Kamand Kojouri, author of *The Eternal Dance*. "There's no greater sin than breaking a heart."

A yogic tradition has it that speech must pass before three gates before being uttered. These gates are in the form of three questions: *Is it kind? Is it true? Is it necessary?*

"Be kind, for everyone you meet is fighting a harder battle," said Plato.

We should try to be the reason someone smiles today. The reason someone feels loved and respected. We all need that feeling.

"Kindness is a language which the deaf can hear and the blind can see," said Mark Twain.

Don't delay kindness, said Ralph Waldo Emerson: "You cannot do a kindness too soon, "for you never know how soon it will be too late."

Here are some beautiful words from Frances Hodgson Burnett, author of *A Little Princess*:

"If nature has made you for a giver, your hands are born open, and so is your heart; and though there may be times when your hands are empty, your heart is always full, and you can give things out of that—warm things, kind things, sweet things—help and comfort and laughter—and sometimes joyful, kind laughter is the best help of all."

During the pandemic, we all saw acts of kindness that we agreed were heroic. Some took great courage, some a big heart, some a huge effort, some as small but as effective as a smile. Kindness touches all of us. We feel it when we give it, when we receive it and even when we see it in others. It's just magical.

Here's what Jennifer Donnelly said about kindness in *Stepsister*:

"There is magic in this sad, hard world. A magic stronger than fate, stronger than chance. And it is seen in the unlikeliest of places. By a hearth at night, as a girl leaves a bit of cheese for a hungry mouse. In a slaughter yard, as the old and infirm, the weak and discarded, are made to matter more than money. In a poor carpenter's small attic room, where three sisters learned that the price of forgiveness is forgiving. And now, on a battlefield, as a mere girl tries to turn the red tide of war. It is the magic of a frail and fallible creature, one capable of both unspeakable cruelty and immense kindness. It lives inside every human being ready to redeem us. To transform us. To save us. If we can only find the courage to listen to it. It is the magic of the human heart."

When a pandemic rages, we see sadness, tragedy, heartbreak, desperation, broken families and all manner of breakdown in the human condition. But, because life is such a struggle, we can more easily recognise courage and selflessness and that magic of the human heart when we see it or experience it.

"It is only with true love and compassion that we can begin to mend what is broken in the world," said Steve Maraboli, author of *Life, the Truth and Being Free*. "It is these two blessed things that can begin to heal all broken hearts."

Sometimes, all we need to do is to sit a while with a friend. Sometimes we might talk, sometimes we just might watch a sunset together while healing starts. Sometimes we just sit in silence while a friend talks.

What do we crave most?

"Do you know what people really want?" said Nobel Prize-winner Doris Lessing. "Everyone, I mean. Everybody in the world is thinking: I wish there was just one other person I could really talk to, who could really understand me, who'd be kind to me. That's what people really want, if they're telling the truth."

In a time of separation and social isolation, isn't that what many of us crave? Human contact. We need to tell our troubles to someone. Someone who will listen. Someone kind.

"But oh! the blessing it is to have a friend to whom one can speak fearlessly on any subject," said Dinah Craik, author of *A Life for a Life*, "with whom one's deepest as well as one's most foolish thoughts come out simply and safely. Oh, the comfort - the inexpressible comfort of feeling safe with a person - having neither to weigh thoughts nor measure words, but pouring them all right out, just as they are, chaff and grain together; certain that a faithful hand will take and sift them, keep what is worth keeping, and then with the breath of kindness blow the rest away."

It only takes one small kindness to change a life, to change our little corner of the world, to change everything for someone. Nothing is more potent for change than small, individual acts of human kindness. Nothing more needed, nothing more appreciated.

"You know, some things don't matter that much... like the colour of a house," said author Sue Monk Kidd. "How big is that in the overall scheme of life? But lifting a person's heart - now, that matters."

Friendship is priceless

Few things in life are worse than loneliness, and you have the power to banish loneliness in those you wish to befriend. Friendship is priceless and can't be bought, but you can give it.

Everyone needs friends, real friends, but we only discover them in times of trouble. Those who no longer want to know us are only fair-weather friends. You can be a foul-weather friend to someone in need.

American broadcaster Walter Winchell said: "A real friend is one who walks in when the rest of the world walks out."

Alaskan Peter Kalifornsky, a Dena'ina elder, said people should live by "choosing one another as friends, to be happy, to joke with one another, and to love one another".

Mother Teresa knows a thing or two about the needs of ordinary people. She ministered to countless numbers of the poor in the streets of Old Calcutta. Here's what she said about reaching out to people: "There is a hunger for ordinary bread, and there is a hunger for love, for kindness, for thoughtfulness; and this is the great poverty that makes people suffer so much."

If you can be sensitive to needs, non-intrusive, caring, attentive, willing to put in the effort, willing to laugh, willing to cry, willing to love - you can be a friend.

You can alleviate this need for love and kindness.

And sometimes - sometimes - a miracle happens. That person becomes your friend and, miracle of miracles, returns the friendship.

Anna Lindsay had this to say in *What is Worthwhile?*:

"A friend gives us confidence for life. A friend makes us outdo ourselves... It is a great and solemn thing to say to another human soul: In this one life that we have to live, we will share all things temporal and spiritual. Your joys shall be my joys. Your sorrows shall be my sorrows. In absence you shall yet be near. You shall never be so far from me but that I can hear your voice in the twilight and in the night-season... To you may I speak the deep thoughts of my heart... To you only can I say: Behold, here I am, an undisguised human soul. All others know me in some one mood - you know me in all moods."

The abundance that is ours

Gifts flow to us from many countries. A Japanese scientist, Kitasato, isolated the bacillus of tetanus. An Austrian, Landsteiner, gave us blood transfusions. A Russian, Metchnikoff, solved the problem of typhoid fever. An Italian, Grassi, did the same for malaria. A Frenchman, Pasteur, and a German, Koch, did the same for surgical infection. They all gave us something special. They gave us life.

Right now, people in many countries are working night and day to find a vaccine for COVID-19.

Someone gave us light and paint and telephones and computer chips and the Internet and cars and hygiene and knowledge of all kinds. We take all these gifts without a thought.

We can never give the world enough to repay all we receive. But it seems to me we should try to give our best. Work a little harder and more diligently, smile more, offer a hand, comfort the sick, ignore the aching back to carry a baby or play with a child. Do more, be more, give more.

Grenville Gleiser said the best thing to give your enemies was forgiveness; to an opponent, tolerance; to a friend, your heart; to your child, a good example; to a father, reverence; to your mother, conduct that will make her proud of you; to yourself, respect; to all mankind, kindness.

Everything we see or feel or smell or touch or hear is either a gift from God or a gift from someone else. Look around. Then, when you do have an opportunity to give, do as poet Walt Whitman did.

"When I give," he said, "I give myself."

Ralph Waldo Emerson summed it all up: "The only gift is a portion of yourself... the poet brings his poem; the shepherd his lamb; the girl, a handkerchief of her own sewing."

In your quiet time now, I hope you can spare a thought for what you owe. Kindness reciprocated or passed on can have unexpected and unimagined consequences. Helene Rubinstein understood the miracle of a small kindness:

"Who can tell when some fragmentary gift of knowledge or wisdom will enrich other lives? Or how a small seed of help, passed from one person to another, may generate something new, something wonderful... a seed which neither the giver nor the receiver can truly evaluate at the time."

As Mahatma Gandhi put it: "The simplest acts of kindness are by far more powerful than a thousand heads bowing in prayer."

I would like to think that, out of the misery of this COVID-19 pandemic, small acts of kindness multiplying all over the world, will create something better than the old world order. A world of compassion and love. Let's be kind when we can. Let's make kindness a habit and a way of life. Let it become an epidemic.

Actress Goldie Hawn knew the transformation power of kindness in troubled times:

"The lotus is the most beautiful flower, whose petals open one by one. But it will only grow in the mud. In order to grow and gain wisdom, first you must have the mud - the obstacles of life and its suffering. The mud speaks of the common ground that humans share, no matter what our stations in life. Whether we have it all or we have nothing, we are all faced with the same obstacles: sadness, loss, illness, dying and death. If we are to strive as human beings to gain more wisdom, more kindness and more compassion, we must have the intention to grow as a lotus and open each petal one by one."

Open like a lotus

So this is what I hope for you: To open like a lotus, one step at a time, one act of compassion and kindness at a time. I hope you can cast aside fears and worries and obstacles to make a better you, one that will be recognised and loved in return.

Let's give the last word on kindness to author Neil Gaiman:

"I hope you will have a wonderful year, that you'll dream dangerously and outrageously, that you will make something that didn't exist before you made it, that you will be loved and that you will be liked, and that you will have people to love and to like in return. And, most importantly (because I think there should be more kindness and more wisdom in the world right now), that you will, when you need to be, be wise, and that you will always be kind."

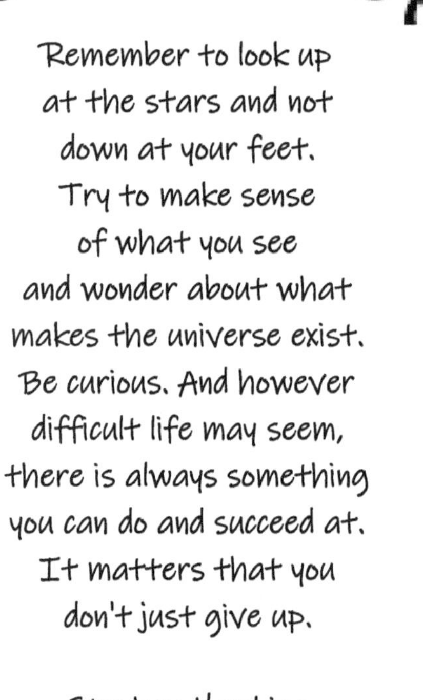
Remember to look up
at the stars and not
down at your feet.
Try to make sense
of what you see
and wonder about what
makes the universe exist.
Be curious. And however
difficult life may seem,
there is always something
you can do and succeed at.
It matters that you
don't just give up.

Stephen Hawking

Life as Service

"Service to other people, especially to the underprivileged, can be a truly inspiring and uplifting experience, a source of real joy."
Dada J. P. Vaswani

"Live your life in such a way that you'll be remembered for your kindness, compassion, fairness, character, benevolence, and a force for good who had much respect for life in general."
Germany Kent

"The greatest purpose in life, the greatest achievement one could ever have in life, the greatest satisfaction one could ever get in life can only be found in the service of others."
Omoakhuana Anthonia

Once upon a time, when I was a boy, I had many heroes, most of them sports people. But there were others (I called them real life heroes) and pioneer anthropologist Margaret Mead was top of the list.

She went to places no-one dared go to live with primitive peoples and study how they lived, what they thought, how they survived. And she discovered things that surprised her and shocked the rest of her normal world.

I read everything she wrote that I could get my hands on and was absolutely enthralled. At an age when I barely understood the world I lived in, Margaret Mead opened up fascinating new worlds of wonder.

One day, she was asked by a student what she thought the first sign of civilisation in a culture might be. The assembled students expected her to talk about things they had heard before, like grinding stones, fishing nets, cooking implements and things that made life easier.

She did not.

This trail-blazing anthropologist said the first sign of civilisation in an ancient culture would be something like a femur, a thighbone, that had broken and healed.

Mead told the stunned students that, if an animal broke a leg, it died. If an animal can't run from a predator or get to water or find food, it can't defend itself and becomes prey for other animals. It could not survive a broken leg long enough for the bone to mend and heal.

The anthropologist said a broken leg that had healed could have only one explanation: Someone had found the injured animal (or person), had helped the animal or person to safety, had probably bound the wound and cared for the injury until it healed.

"Helping someone else through difficulty is where civilization starts," Mead told the students.

It's my contention that helping someone through a pandemic is what makes heroes during it and a better world after it.

A better life can be built for oneself through service to others. In a troubled world, it might be the only way to self-satisfaction.

As Leo Tolstoy put it: "Joy can only be real if people look upon their life as a service and have a definite object in life outside themselves and their personal happiness."

Yes, a life of service brings joy plus a sense of self-worth.

Pay back the goodness

Let me tell you a little of my own beliefs, my philosophy of life. I believe we should earn the right to be here. Here in a family, in a community, in a job, in a country, on this planet.

Wherever we are, we cannot possibly repay all the goodness and benefits that flow to us.

Instead of just taking things for granted, we ought to try to make wherever we are a little better than we found it.

I would not swap the inner satisfaction I get from practising this simple philosophy for any of the "riches" the world treasures.

The secret is to give

If we want a better world, if we want a better life, we have to find a way to give. We have to find empathy and reach out beyond our comfort zone to provide better service and more comfort to those whose paths we cross.

Compassionate service is the path to tackling problems in our families, our communities, our country, our world.

"Making the earth a better place for humans needs people with hearts full of mercy, full of love towards humanity, persons who have a high sense of responsibility, and live consciences," said children's author, Noora Anmed Alsuwaidi. "Be one of them, and support anyone who is like them."

People of all religions (and many who have none at all) love the work of Mother Teresa in India as founder of the Missionaries of Charity.

She is now called Saint Teresa, but many who knew her and lived with her still call her Mother.

"I alone cannot change the world," she said, "but I can cast a stone across the water to create many ripples. And, if I can't feed a hundred people, I can feed just one."

We all can't be a Saint Teresa, but we will, in the new world after the pandemic, have to summon the same spirit and the same courage to do what we can to make that world better. We might need to find the spirit, sooner or later, to fight for a cause, for freedom, for honour, for the common good, for a friend, for ourselves.

We don't know what the future holds, but we must be ready to face it, for ourselves and our families.

Soon after we were married, my wife presented the world with a beautiful baby girl and we began to think of the world we wanted for her. We settled on a town on the outskirts of Sydney, Campbelltown. This town was programmed to grow quickly to city status and we thought it would be a good place to raise a family.

When we moved in, however, we found that there was only one ambulance for the rapidly expanding population. This was alarming, but a community fund-raising campaign had started for another ambulance and we pitched in. The campaign was successful, but it was just the start of nearly 50 years of community service for us in and around Campbelltown.

A new hospital came and a university and an expanded police station and courthouse and a Sheltered Workshop for the Disabled, and many helpful projects we became involved with. Wherever we have lived and wherever you live, there has been and always will be the need for people of goodwill to help, to do what they can.

Wherever there is a need, there is an opportunity for people like you and me to do our share. I think it's a responsibility we must accept in whatever way we can.

Gloom or bloom

You might have to fight off defeat, or, when you do suffer defeat, fight against the bitterness of it and get on with living. As we said earlier, when you're going through hell, you have no option – you have to keep going.

I'm quite sure the "old normal" will come back in more ways than many of us like. Greed will be back, as will injustice, inequality, crimes against humanity and so much more that we didn't like first time around. There will be those will think only of themselves and will seek to exploit the vulnerable. And, of course, there will be politicians doing what they can get away with until enough people get fed up and change things at elections.

We can't change the world, but we can change *our* world and our place in it. If we say this often enough, it will become our motto.

Once again, we will have to triumph over anger, bear up under loss, smile when the tears well up, fight evil of every kind - whether it be a disease (like a pandemic) or the base instincts of the human race or evil people themselves.

At the same time, we must be at peace within ourselves and, as far as possible, with people around us. We must find a way to be the best we can be in the new world.

Strength to live the good life goes hand-in-hand with courage. I want you to find strength when you need it - all kinds of strength: strength of will, strength of compassion, strength in your convictions.

I have come to know the Children's Hospital at Westmead (Sydney) through visits with children and grandchildren and through membership of a community service organization when we tried to bring cheer to sick children. If you spend a little time at Westmead, you won't forget it.

Time after time, I found myself wandering the corridors, poking my head in ward doorways, watching those kids.

So many of them.

Many had bald heads, of course. Some with scarves over their heads. Most with dark, sad eyes. Tubes seemed to be keeping them alive. They mostly reclined on the beds and seemed so calm.

How could they be so calm? What strength did they have, and where did they find it? Some were smiling, somehow, or even laughing with brothers, sisters, parents.

I'm not sure where the trolleys came from, but mothers found them. They'd bundle their children onto a trolley and take them for a walk - along the corridors or out into the gardens and sunshine. They looked so frail, those mothers, and the trolleys were not easy to push, but mothers have strength they don't know they have until their children need it.

Inside the hospital, a little chapel offered sanctuary. It was small and smelled of furniture polish, rather than incense. It was clearly a place of refuge for parents and loved ones, struggling to cope with the tragedy that had befallen their family. I spent time in there, too, mostly just sitting and watching the mothers shuffling in. How weary they looked. Surely they had no strength for words to pray, but they'd sit there for a while quietly, and then, with a sigh, stand and walk out again to whatever they had to face.

I did not have the strength of those mothers, and I doubt that I could have coped with what I had seen without the sanctity and serenity of that chapel.

If you have strength when you are young, you are fortunate, but I think you'll find that strength grows with the years and something magical happens. I don't think you can be old while you still have strength.

So, look for strength within yourself: strength to endure grief, strength to hang on after tragedy, strength to never bow your head before the forces of might or cruelty or injustice. Strength to rise above the daily grind, strength to persevere, strength to serve with love. Strength of body, yes, but also of mind.

Real strength.

Sometimes the great writers come up with a few words that offer real strength to their readers. Listen to Victor Hugo:

"Have courage for the great sorrows of life and patience for the small ones; and when you have laboriously accomplished your daily task, go to sleep in peace. God is awake."

I've read those words several times, but the significance of those last three words, "God is awake", has only just hit me. What a comfort they must be for so many of us.

Humanity needs your spirit

In times of trouble, many of us are surprised to find there is a noble spirit residing in us and we want to use whatever skills we have to be useful - to make our corner of the world a little bit better than we found it.

The world conspires to fill our lives with busyness - especially in the age of the Internet and smart phones. We can easily be swamped in a landslide of trivia. If our worlds are so empty that we need to fill them with things that do not matter, surely we are in desperate need of something greater than ourselves to fill that space instead?

Buckminster Fuller was a futurist and a hero to many when I was growing up. "There is no joy equal to that of being able to work for all humanity and doing what you're doing well," he said.

Whatever you do might be insignificant, but, as Mahatma Gandhi said, it is very important that you do it. And do it as well as you are able. Hold on to hope and look for the good in humanity.

"You must not lose faith in humanity," Gandhi said. "Humanity is an ocean; if a few drops of the ocean are dirty, the ocean does not become dirty."

If the new world is unjust, as the old one was, then let us be dissidents.

"Since the world has existed, there has been injustice," said Audrey Hepburn, actor and UNICEF Goodwill Ambassador. "But it is one world, the more so as it becomes smaller, more accessible. There is just no question that there is more obligation that those who have should give to those who have nothing."

I am one of many whose blood boils at the sight of injustice. We fight it at every opportunity. I've been active in protests and organisations standing up for human rights, but my main weapon has always been my pen. These days, physical disability makes it my only weapon. In 2018, my years of service was recognized when I was designated a Global Goodwill Ambassador pledged to support and stand up for the United Nations Sustainable Development Goals in Human Rights.

The seventeen U.N. sustainable development goals to transform our world offer opportunities, big and small, for all of us.

You might have a particular interest in one or more of these goals:

GOAL 1: No Poverty
GOAL 2: Zero Hunger
GOAL 3: Good Health and Well-being
GOAL 4: Quality Education
GOAL 5: Gender Equality
GOAL 6: Clean Water and Sanitation
GOAL 7: Affordable and Clean Energy
GOAL 8: Decent Work and Economic Growth
GOAL 9: Industry, Innovation and Infrastructure
GOAL 10: Reduced Inequality
GOAL 11: Sustainable Cities and Communities
GOAL 12: Responsible Consumption and Production
GOAL 13: Climate Action
GOAL 14: Life Below Water
GOAL 15: Life on Land
GOAL 16: Peace and Justice, Strong Institutions
GOAL 17: Partnerships to achieve the Goals.

Throughout the world, in ways large and small, there are opportunities to work towards some of these goals. In developing countries, of course, the need is great, but even in advanced economies, there are problems like poverty, hunger, poor health, inequality, unfairness and, the big one, climate change and the environment. I think we can all find little ways to help if we keep out eyes open.

You might think that one person can't do much. But every drop makes the ocean greater. You don't have to have special qualifications, you just have to be human.

How should you be valued?

"Everyone needs to be valued," said Princess Diana. "Everyone has the potential to give something back."

Life's most persistent and urgent question is the one Martin Luther King Jr asked: "What are you doing for others?"

If we want our lives to mean something, perhaps we should worry less about what we have and think instead about what we can give. I don't sleep very well, but there are some nights when I rest much easier. Those are the nights when I have felt really good because I've helped someone.

The way I look at it, I can't do all the good the world needs, but the world needs what good I *can* do.

There is no greater work on this world than to help the helpless. What greater quest is there than to bring hope to the hopeless? What greater achievement than to lift the fallen?

Feeling weary right now? The best cure for weariness is to carry a load for someone who is even more weary. It's a fact of life that the person who helps nearly always benefits more than the person being helped.

You know, the prayers we *say* will often contribute to our happiness and our peace of mind, but of even more importance might be the prayers we *answer.*

"I don't know what your destiny will be," said the beloved Albert Schweitzer, "but one thing I know: the only ones among you who will be really happy are those who have sought and found how to serve."

My objective in writing this book is to suggest ways, as we struggle out of a terrible pandemic, that we might look at our lives to make them better. As I write this, I'm on my 81st orbit of the sun, so I've been around for a while and would really like you to consider something that has made my life content and, for the most part, free of regret. Service. Make your life a life of service and you will never regret it.

But I'm just one voice. Let's finish this chapter with three voices I know you love and respect.

J.K. Rowling:

"The power of human empathy, leading to collective action, saves lives and frees prisoners. Ordinary people, whose personal well-being and security are assured, join together in huge numbers to save people they do not know, and will never meet… Unlike any other creature on this planet, humans can learn and understand, without having experienced. They can think themselves into other people's places… We need no magic

to change the world, we carry all the power we need inside ourselves already: we have the power to imagine better."

Saint Teresa:

"At the end of life we will not be judged by how many diplomas we have received, how much money we have made, how many great things we have done.

"We will be judged by 'I was hungry, and you gave me something to eat, I was naked and you clothed me. I was homeless, and you took me in'."

George Bernard Shaw:

"This is the true joy in life, the being used for a purpose recognized by yourself as a mighty one; the being a force of nature instead of a feverish, selfish little clod of ailments and grievances complaining that the world will not devote itself to making you happy.

I am of the opinion that my life belongs to the whole community, and as long as I live it is my privilege to do for it whatever I can.

I want to be thoroughly used up when I die, for the harder I work the more I live. I rejoice in life for its own sake. Life is no 'brief candle' for me. It is a sort of splendid torch which I have got hold of for the moment, and I want to make it burn as brightly as possible before handing it on to future generations."

So, go now and be a blessing to the world and a joy to your family.

Often
what may appear
as a detour in life
is actually the most
direct and empowering
path to your
destination.

James Arthur Ray

Your quest for a better life

"There are far, far better things ahead
than any we leave behind."
C.S. Lewis

"Breathe. Let go. And remind yourself
that this very moment is the only one
you know you have for sure."
Oprah Winfrey

"Be who you are and say what you feel,
because those who mind don't matter
and those who matter don't mind."
Dr. Seuss

"When I hear somebody sigh,
'Life is hard,'
I am always tempted to ask,
'Compared to what?'"
Sydney Harris

I have had a blessed life – and I can thank my wife, Judy, for that. A few years ago, I was feeling very grateful for everything in my life. I felt I was the richest bloke on the planet, although money riches seemed to have passed me by. Other things have always been more important to me, which was probably not a good thing for my family.

However, I was feeling very loved and I wanted others to feel that, too. Life is so full of abundance and blessings, and, as Louis Armstrong sang: "It's a wonderful world."

I felt I was the richest man in the world. I wanted to write about these things and for people to realise just how rich they were.

So, I wrote a little book, called *You Are Already Rich: Riches Beyond Your Dreams, Treasures Beyond Your Imaginings*. In it, I set out the wonders of the "twelve rooms" of your treasure house and how we were all entitled to share in this wealth.

However, I wrote, just as there is a Codicil in a Last Will and Testament, there is fine print in the Book of Life. There's always fine print, isn't there? Goethe said it best: *"The possessions you have inherited - earn them in order to truly own them."*

Because you have been a worthy citizen of this world, you are entitled to all the inheritance, named and unnamed, in the vast treasury of this planet.

Heed the words of Joseph Murphy, who believed that you already hold great riches within you:

"Infinite riches are all around you if you will open your mental eyes and behold the treasure house of infinity within you. There is a gold mine within you from which you can extract everything you need to live gloriously, joyously, and abundantly."

Many of us want a better life, but just don't see how close that better life awaits.

Remember Anna Quindlen? "I read and walked for miles at night along the beach," she said, "writing bad blank verse and searching endlessly for someone wonderful who would step out of the darkness and change my life. It never crossed my mind that that person could be me."

So many riches are yours for the taking, just by being open to them. As Henry David Thoreau put it, the setting sun is reflected from the windows of the poorhouse as brightly as from the rich man's abode.

There is so much just sitting there, free, waiting for you and your family.

As a matter of fact, I felt a little poetry coming upon me as I wrote. A little something from Omar Khayyam:

A gourd of wine and a sheaf of poems,
A bare subsistence, half a loaf, no more,
Supplies us two alone in the free desert:
What sultan would we envy on his throne?

Indeed.

Absorb life's bounty

I know full well that life is not always a bed of roses. We all know that after suffering during the pandemic. But, if we look for and absorb into our lives the richness that is all about us, we can be happier and more fulfilled and brimming with hope.

I think a greater poverty than that caused by lack of money is the poverty of unawareness of what's around us.

"Men and women go about the world unaware of the beauty, the goodness, and the glories in it," said Jerry Fleishman. "Their souls are poor. It's better to have a poor pocketbook than to suffer from a poor soul."

However, as the great writer Isak Dinesen said: "Difficult times have helped me to understand better than before how infinitely rich and beautiful life is in every way, and that so many things that one goes worrying about are of no consequence whatsoever."

Would you like to be money rich, or would you like to be loved and respected? I don't see why you can't strive for both, but here's what Archibald Rutledge had to say:

"You should remember that, though another may have more money, beauty and brains than you, yet, when it comes to the rarer spiritual values such as charity, self-sacrifice, honour, nobility of heart, you have an equal chance with anyone to be the most beloved and honoured of all people."

Cling to your dreams. Absorb the abundance of life. Eleanor Roosevelt saw much of life and summed it up: "The future belongs to those who believe in the beauty of the dream."

Yes, dream.

"Twenty years from now you will be more disappointed by the things you didn't do than by the ones you did," said Mark Twain. "So throw off the bowlines, sail away from the safe harbour. Catch the trade winds in your sails. Explore. Dream."

A heart full of riches

You are entitled to all the riches a heart can hold; all the blessings a soul can hold dear.

Well, almost. I, personally, am the richest person on earth because of all that I revealed in my book - plus something extra. Something extra that I can't give away, even to you.

I have my family. I have special friends. I have the love they have showered on me; I have the luxury and the felicity of their presence in my life. I cannot give that to you directly even in death.

Each of us must give and receive our own love.

In the meantime, though you now enjoy the gifts of a lifetime, they come with two strings attached. Ah, there's that fine print again.

Firstly, you are charged with the responsibility of preserving all of these riches, and enhancing them if you can. This wealth must not be squandered.

Australian aboriginal writer, Burnum Burnum, said modern ecology could learn a great deal from the Aboriginal people who managed and maintained their world so well for fifty thousand years.

Air, earth, water - the essentials of life are to be enhanced, not depleted. If you cannot or will not preserve all of your inheritance offered to you in this world - all of it - you must leave it for others who will.

Secondly, you are also charged with the responsibility of passing on riches to others, so that future generations will have their share of life's bounty. And what bounty it will be - your own dearly-held possessions combined with the vast holdings of our combined treasuries.

Share the wealth you reap

Oren Lyons, who glories in the wonderful title of Onondaga Faithkeeper, said that, in his people's way of life, with every decision they make, they always keep in mind the seventh generation to come.

"It's our job to see that the people coming ahead, the generations still unborn, have a world no worse than ours - and hopefully better," he said.

"When we walk upon Mother Earth we always plant our feet carefully because we know the faces of our future generations are looking up at us from beneath the ground. We never forget them."

Seems to me that this combined wealth, should you choose to accept the gifts that are yours for the taking, would make you one of the richest people on earth - but you must be willing to share it.

Big hearts are made for giving

A Papua New Guinea elder, speaking to author Anne Wilson Schaef, said: "I am a big man. See all these shells? They are very valuable in our culture. I could have trunks of them... but then I wouldn't be a big man. A big man gives away what he has and shares with others."

Let me tell you a little story about sharing.

A man wandered for days in the Australian bush, becoming weaker and weaker. Heat, hunger and thirst had almost done him in when an Aboriginal found him. The Aboriginal led him to a shady tree burdened with fruit. The tree was watered by a nearby spring. The exhausted man offered profuse thanks to the Aboriginal, who smiled and walked off.

The man drank from the spring and filled his water-bottle. He ate the fruit and rested in the shade until he regained his strength.

As he finally left, the man looked back at the tree.

"How can I thank the tree that saved me?" he thought. "It has everything: plentiful water, luscious fruit, life-saving shade."

Then he turned to the heavens and said: "Give this tree one final blessing. May the birds of the air carry its seeds to other places and may they flourish, multiplying the gifts of the tree."

May the gifts of your inheritance multiply and flow to others. May you, as the Buddha put it, drink deeply and live in serenity and joy.

Thrive. Be authentic

Our mission in life should be the same as Maya Angelou's: "My mission in life is not merely to survive, but to thrive; and to do so with some passion, some compassion, some humour, and some style."

So, let's thrive.

We all write the stories of our own lives. Our life tells the story of what our families mean to us, how we care, what we give, what we do for others. Our story, or the parts that matter, talk about kindness and how we laugh together and what we go through together.

Real stuff. Things that matter. Love, honesty, courage, truth, morals. People we love. Things of value. We want our story to be about the things in our lives that create the feelings, the emotions, that seep deep into our psyche.

Our lives have to be authentic. Moral authority comes from integrity. If we let goodness, truth and integrity pervade how we live, our authenticity will be recognized.

As we come out of this pandemic, we are joining people around the world who are striving to make themselves better people and to use their skills and experience to help create a better world. The two - making ourselves better and making our lives better - go hand-in-hand.

It's a choice we make.

With this attitude to life and living, how can we not produce more useful, more beneficial work, and work that is appreciated and helpful to others?

If we seek honesty and look for the values and principles that we find worthwhile, then we are taking the integrity road.

It's the road that leads to a life of service and that brings joy and a wonderful sense of self-worth.

As we discussed, we have to find empathy and reach out beyond our comfort zone to provide better service and wiser, more useful help to those around us.

Compassionate service is the path to tackling problems in our families, our communities, our country, our world.

Past, Present, Future

So here we are. Reflecting on our times, on the past with all its faults and the future with all its promise. And, as we reflect on the past and the future, we also think of the present with its opportunity for a beautiful, rich and slower lifestyle.

We are finding that time is not and should not be defined by the clock. We need to be present in the present.

Tragedy has brought us to the here and now. A pandemic that threw the world into chaos and a soul-destroying death that threw the world into a Black Deaths Matter protest. A protest that seemed to cry out for, not only a Black Death, terrible as it was, but also a loss of civility and justice and equality in the world.

We see things with different eyes now. We need to stop for a moment and breathe.

This blue planet is going through a series of crises. A pandemic worse than we have experienced in our lifetimes. A rise of mostly peaceful warriors in protest. And climate change that will destroy all our dreams and all of humanity if we let it continue.

As individuals, we surely must view these crises as an opportunity. An opportunity to reshape our thinking about our own lives and our future on this planet. An opportunity to live our lives with the whole of humankind in our vision.

So, as we struggle out of this pandemic, with serious concerns all around us, we have an opportunity to try for something extraordinary. We can change our little corner of the world and join millions of others pledging themselves to live better and to do the same. We can create our own world of love, of kindness, of respect for the one and only race – the human race.

And so we'll work for the many small changes that will make the whole world a better place.

Let us thrive in the life we choose to live. Let us fill our hearts and then open them to the world.

Our destiny, surely, our mission in life, is to serve and to thrive. To do what we can.

So let's begin. Let's live. Let's thrive. And may the wind be forever at your back.

EPILOGUE 1
Bonus story

The Story of Desiderata

This is the first of two bonus stories that complement *After the Storm* in one way or another.

It's the story of the poem that travelled around the world and encouraged millions of people who were lifted by the inspiring words. And we could all do with a bit of a lift during this pandemic, right?

You have probably read this poem or heard it recorded by various celebrities, but sometimes we need to revisit words so lovingly crafted.

In your search for a better life beyond COVID-19, I hope you enjoy *Desiderata,* which follows the story of its journey to you.

Let me tell you the story of this beautiful prose poem, *Desiderata,* that has meant so much to so many people.

I believe it has a powerful message for each of us in today's complex world of uncertainty during a pandemic.

The name, *Desiderata,* comes from the Latin and means "things that are desired" and American writer, Max Ehrmann, said he wrote it for himself, rather than for publication.

"I wrote it for myself," he said, "because it counsels those virtues I felt I needed most."

Sometimes a writer has to get down on paper whatever is consuming his heart and soul day in and day out. This was such a time for Max Ehrmann.

He was struggling, as we are now, with finding a way out of unsettling and difficult times. Survivors of World War I were home at long last and people everywhere were looking for a better way of living.

Massive technology advances changed almost every aspect of life. Cars, mass production and aviation made change the norm. Conflicts still raged between nations, as between Britain and China, and natural disasters, like the massive flood in America, disrupted life for many.

The world was still recovering from the Spanish Flu pandemic that infected one third of the world's population between 1918 and 1920.

And wildly fluctuating world economies were soon to lose a battle that ended in the Great Depression a few years later.

We were not the first to suffer a pandemic and tough times. And not the first to seek a better life.

Even so, Max Ehrmann was perhaps a man ahead of his time, because, however much it meant to him, the poem was largely unknown in his lifetime. Today, though, it resonates with people all around the world. Today, those virtues and the thoughts the poet expressed are sorely needed by many of us, as we discussed in *After the Storm*.

Desiderata has attracted many myths over the years, including the belief that it was written in the 17th century. It wasn't. It was penned in 1927, not all that long ago in the grand scheme of things.

Whatever way you look at it, this poem has not grown out of fashion in any way. In fact, its importance has soared as the world changed.

Here is a little of is history.

Ehrmann registered the words on January 3, 1927, under the copyright number A962402.

He probably wrote it as a gift to himself and his wife, Bertha, for Christmas in 1926.

Unfortunately for his family, the copyright was later forfeited.

Desiderata was not published when it was written in 1927, but, 15 years later, Max Ehrmann did permit its circulation. In 1942, he allowed copies to be distributed to soldiers to boost morale during World War II.

It's easy to imagine battle-hardened soldiers drawing comfort from the words in times of respite.

The poet died in 1945 and, three years later, his widow, Bertha K. Ehrmann, included *Desiderata* in *The Poems of Max Ehrmann*, published in Boston.

In 1954, she renewed the copyright.

She clearly wanted the words to remain in the family.

Two years later, the Reverend Frederick Kates published a collection of devotional materials for his congregation, including *Desiderata* and his church's foundation date - Old Saint Paul's Church, Baltimore AD 1692.

As a result, readers assumed the poem was written in that year, 1692. Some people still think this is true.

In 1967, Robert L. Bell acquired the publishing rights from the Boston publishing house, where he was president. By then, the poet's nephew, Richard Wright, had inherited the copyright in his uncle's written works and he sold the *Desiderata* rights to Robert Bell.

In August 1971, the poem was published in the famous *Success Unlimited* magazine, without Bell's permission. Bell started litigation and, in 1976, the court ruled that copyright had been forfeited because the poem had been authorized for publication without a copyright notice in the 1940s - and the poem was therefore in the public domain.

Copyright was lost and *Desiderata* could be freely published in any form. Celebrities, in particular, started to create their own versions and people began to love the poem.

When US Democratic presidential candidate Adlai Stevenson passed away in 1965, a copy of *Desiderata* was found in his bedroom. Stevenson had planned to use the words in his Christmas cards. When this news began to be featured in the media, *Desiderata's* fame spread.

In the 1960s and 1970s, *Desiderata* was widely distributed in poster form.

Leonard Nimoy, of *Star Trek* fame, recited the poem in his 1968 album, *Two Sides of Leonard Nimoy*. He called it *Spock Thoughts* and it also appeared in a 1995 recording by the actor.

(Nimoy changed the ending from "Be cheerful" to "Be careful" and others followed his lead, believing "careful" to be the correct word).

It was a case of world-famous interviewer meeting world-famous actress early in 1970, when David Frost interviewed Joan Crawford for television. The interview might have been forgotten, but Crawford won hearts at the end of it by reciting *Desiderata*.

Music and song usually crowd the popular charts, but, in 1971 and 1972, a spoken-word recording hit the charts. Les Crane's *Desiderata,* on his Warner Bros. album of the same name, raced up the lists in the U.S., the U.K., Canada and Australia. This version was recreated 40 years later in German by country music singer Carl Emroy.

Many other performances followed.

Politicians don't often recite poetry, but Canada's Pierre Trudeau reassured the nation that "the universe is unfolding as it should" when his government lost its majority in 1972.

When he lost power altogether seven years later, he resorted to *Desiderata's* final stanza.

The poem was also pirated – but in a good way.

Israeli radio station owner Abie Nathan called his radio show the *Voice of Peace.* It was broadcast from a pirate radio ship "somewhere in the Mediterranean".

As a special feature, every evening he recited *Desiderata* and his audience loved it.

There were many other versions of the poem over the years in many countries and the words were treasured everywhere.

These days, Max Ehrmann is remembered in his hometown, Terre Haute, Indiana. In 2010, a bronze statue, sculpted by Bill Wolfe, was unveiled there, showing Ehrmann sitting on a park bench. People walking by can read lines of his poem as they pass.

The poet often sat on this bench during his lifetime, taking to heart his own words: "Go placidly amid the noise and haste." He was thinking and observing life around him as inspiration for his writing.

Beautiful words, assembled by a master writer, can leave an indelible mark on readers' hearts and can even change lives, as *Desiderata* has done.

I hope the virtues and thoughts expressed as long ago will touch you as deeply as they did Max Ehrmann, when he wrote them for himself in troubled times.

Be cheerful. Strive to be happy.

Brian Morgan

DESIDERATA

Max Ehrmann

Go placidly amid the noise and haste,
and remember what peace there may be in silence.
As far as possible without surrender
be on good terms with all persons.

Speak your truth quietly and clearly;
and listen to others,
even the dull and the ignorant;
they, too, have their story.

Avoid loud and aggressive persons,
they are vexations to the spirit.
If you compare yourself with others,
you may become vain and bitter;
for always there will be greater and lesser persons
than yourself.

Enjoy your achievements as well as your plans.
Keep interested in your own career, however humble
it is a real possession in the changing fortunes of time.
Exercise caution in your business affairs;
for the world is full of trickery.

But let this not blind you to what virtue there is;
many persons strive for high ideals;
and everywhere life is full of heroism.

Be yourself.
Especially, do not feign affection.
Neither be cynical about love;
for in the face of all aridity and disenchantment
it is as perennial as the grass.

Take kindly the counsel of the years,
gracefully surrendering the things of youth.

Nurture strength of spirit to shield you in sudden misfortune.
But do not distress yourself with dark imaginings.
Many fears are born of fatigue and loneliness.
Beyond a wholesome discipline,
be gentle with yourself.

You are a child of the universe,
no less than the trees and the stars;
you have a right to be here.
And whether or not it is clear to you,
no doubt the universe is unfolding as it should.

Therefore be at peace with God,
whatever you conceive Him to be,
and whatever your labors and aspirations,
in the noisy confusion of life keep peace with your soul.

With all its sham, drudgery, and broken dreams,
it is still a beautiful world.

Be cheerful.
Strive to be happy.

EPILOGUE 2
Bonus story

Walking in Beauty

This is the second of two bonus stories that complement *After the Storm* in one way or another.

The first told the story of one man and his search for a better life. This time, a whole nation faced almost insurmountable problems and turned to their elders, the wisdom-keepers, to find a way out.

The wisdom-keepers sat down to talk and uncovered a secret that had seldom been discussed: that the possibility of a better external world depended on what sat quietly in individual breasts.

Individual minds and hearts held the ingredients to create a beautiful life and a better world. As we found in our quest for a way out of a pandemic, the elders spoke of courage, personal values, integrity, beauty and inner peace.

First the story, then the words of the Beauty Way.

Let's walk with the Navajo.

There is a story about hope in a time of despair that I've known about for a long time, and now is the time to tell it. In the Navajo language it's a *Háâne' Baadahoste' ígíí* (a very sacred story), so I had some difficulty deciding how to tell it.

I had to find a way to treat the story with respect and dignity as befitting the Navajo people, so, in the end, I decided to tell it as the Navajo might, although their tradition is an oral one. I can't tell the whole Navajo story, of course, but I can tell a small part of it – the part that particularly relates to us in a time of pandemic.

It might help to know how other people faced devastation and death, and managed to find a way out. A way that worked so well for them that it still guides their philosophy and lifestyle centuries later.

Perhaps we could learn from them as we seek a life beyond the pandemic.

The Navajo set up their lodges in the American Southwest about six hundred years ago and they are now recognised as one of the biggest, if not the biggest tribe in America. Their Reservation covers land in the Four Corners area of New Mexico, Arizona and Utah.

They believe their Holy Ones placed them between the four sacred mountains: Mt. Hesperus in Colorado, Mt. Blanca and Mt. Taylor in New Mexico and San Francisco Peak, though the boundaries of the Reservation are now smaller than this area.

In our lives, we have been through some tough times, culminating in the pandemic, and this will help us understand the tortured history of the Navajo people with attacks by European settlers and ill-treatment by the United States Federal Government.

That history is well documented, but some appalling scenes stand out.

In the 1860s, Kit Carson was ordered to subdue the Navajo and to force their surrender. Carson and his force stormed the Navajo land and wreaked havoc. They burned dwellings to the ground, destroyed crops (including corn crops considered sacred to the Navajo), fouled the wells and took away the livestock.

Facing starvation and death, the first Navajo straggled into Fort Defiance for water and relief.

Not all Navajo surrendered, but the nation was broken and the trouble did not end for those who had surrendered.

What became known as the Long Walk of the Navajo started in the spring of 1864, when the U.S. Army forced thousands of Navajo men, women, and children to walk more than 300 miles (480 km) to Fort Sumner, New Mexico, to be detained at Bosque Redondo.

The internment at Bosque Redondo was disastrous. The government failed to provide an adequate supply of water, provisions, livestock and wood for the survivors there. Crop failure and disease also hit at this time, and the settlers were subjected to raids by other native tribes and by U.S. civilians.

Some Navajo died, frozen to death, as winter hit, because they were given insufficient materials to make adequate shelter.

Navajo still refer to this as "The Fearing Time". It lasted four years before a treaty finally allowed the Navajo to return to part of their former land.

The Long Walk of the Navajo claimed seven thousand lives, including women and children, and broke many more hearts.

Atrocities and shameful treatment continued to plague the people until March 2020, when COVID-19 invaded the Reservation. As of July 2020, nearly 7000 people have been infected and more than 300 have died. This is an infection rate higher than many states.

Two, three and four generations live in many of the homes on the Reservation, so the virus spread easily. One in every three homes has no access to running water and no electricity, so washing hands and staving off infection remains very difficult on the Reservation.

But here's the thing. Many of the Navajo people refuse to talk of themselves as victims. Life might be tough and uncertain, but they prefer to remain positive and keep hope alive.

No matter what they face, they try to live balanced lives, based on ancestor methods dreamed up long ago.

That's the Navajo way. That's the Beauty Way. A Navajo/Diné traditional prayer is called just that - "The Beauty Way" – and here's how it came to be.

About four hundred years ago, the wisdom-keepers of the Navajo people sat down together in the high desert country of the American Southwest. They were sorely troubled.

They were besieged on all sides by multiple problems and were struggling to survive. Extremes of climate left the people dealing with ferocious heat and bitter cold.

Crops failed and other tribes were a constant menace and attacked frequently.

The wisdom-keepers sought a way out of their troubles into a better, more peaceful life. What they came up with was a series of ceremonies called Blessingway.

Blessingway was, and is, the centre piece of a complex system of Navajo healing ceremonies known as sings, or chants, that was designed to restore balance and equilibrium to individual lives and to the world.

Anthropologists grouped these ceremonies into six major ways, or divisions: the Blessingways, Holyways, Lifeways, Evilways, War Ceremonials, and Gameways. Parts of the Blessingway, especially the songs, are vital to most Navajo ceremonies.

Some healing ceremonies are aimed directly at curing illness, but most Blessingways rituals are designed to invoke positive feelings and are used to induce joyful blessings and to avert misfortune.

As a part of all Navajo religious practices, the Blessingway is considered to be a highly spiritual, sacred, and private event.

A major part of these ceremonies, the Beauty Way is derived from Hózhó, the Navajo concept of living in an atmosphere of beauty, balance, harmony and well-being – an atmosphere not unlike the environment we are trying to generate in this book.

Beauty, in this sense, does not relate to surface appearance and aesthetics. The wisdom-keepers had in mind the essence of beauty. They developed the Beauty Way to cultivate awareness of surroundings, the intention of good works and right conduct, a sense of community, a truly spiritual practice and good feelings generated by ceremonies.

The Navajo were to be nourished by such principles and values as they walked the path of life together. Walking the Beauty Way was to live harmoniously with all of life as it unfolds, however it unfolds. This sense of harmony was to include both the sacred and the natural world. It was to embrace individual lives, their loved ones and their communities.

Life was to be lived with courage, but with peace of mind and serenity at heart.

Navajo traditions have built on these principles.

For centuries, this is how the Navajo people have tried to live and have lived. Perhaps we could learn from this as we seek something better beyond the pandemic for ourselves and our families.

As the Navajo would say: May you walk in beauty all the days of your life.

Brian Morgan

Walking in Beauty

The closing prayer from the
Navajo Way Blessing Ceremony

In beauty I walk
With beauty before me I walk
With beauty behind me I walk
With beauty above me I walk
With beauty around me I walk
It has become beauty again.

Today I will walk out.
Today everything negative will leave me.
I will be as I was before.
I will have a cool breeze over my body.
I will have a light body.
I will be happy forever.
Nothing will hinder me.
I walk with beauty before me.
I walk with beauty behind me.
I walk with beauty below me.
I walk with beauty above me.
I walk with beauty around me.
My words will be beautiful.

In beauty all day long may I walk.
Through the returning seasons may I walk.
On the trail marked with pollen may I walk.
With dew about my feet may I walk.
With beauty before me may I walk.
With beauty behind me may I walk.
With beauty below me may I walk.
With beauty above me may I walk.
With beauty all around me may I walk.

In old age wandering on a trail of beauty,
lively,
may I walk.
In old age wandering on a trail of beauty,
living again,
may I walk.
Words will be beautiful...

Note: For Navajo, pollen is the life source and the pollen path is the path to the centre, to balance in life.

May you walk in beauty all the days of your life

Messages from the author

Three quick messages and then I'll send you on your way to create your better life beyond COVID-19.

First, I'd like to know whether you plan to make that better life and how you plan to do it. You might have ideas that could enhance an updated version of this book later on.

In addition, you might have ideas I or we can share on social media. I have contact details below. You could message me and I could share with others. The more we help each other the better, right?

Secondly, I would really appreciate any help I can get if you think this book could help others. You might have ways of letting people know about it through your various networks (family, friends, work etc.) or through social media.

I would love the opportunity to send you a small gift if you could help and let me know about it.

Unless you are a writer, you probably don't understand the importance of reviews to spread the message of a book, any book, these days.

A review is a great way to let others know whether or not they should buy the book.

Much of a writer's life is spent in solitude and silence. We need all the friends we can get.

Reviews or comments on social media would be simply wonderful and very much appreciated. Comments via email or LinkedIn or Facebook (or other social media) would also be great and could be shared if appropriate.

End of sales pitch. Thank you for anything you can do to get the word out there.

Thirdly, I love to hear what readers think, good or bad. It all helps.

"Writers shouldn't fear criticism," author Robert Fanney said. "Instead, they should fear silence. Criticism is healthy. It gets people thinking about your work and, even better, it gets them talking and arguing. But as for silence - it is the greatest killer of writers. So, if you hate a book and really want to hurt it, don't talk about it. And if you hate my books - please, for God's sake, shout it from the hills!"

Well, I'd kind of prefer a whisper, but I'll leave that to you.

In any event, I want to stay in touch. If I can help you in some way, I'd love to do so.

We can all learn from one another on this journey out of a pandemic and we are all blessed by living in this wonderful world of communication. Let's make use of it. This is one author who would like to be a friend.

In *Catcher in the Rye,* J.D. Salinger said: "What really knocks me out is a book that, when you're all done reading it, you wish the author that wrote it was a terrific friend of yours and you could call him up on the phone whenever you felt like it. That doesn't happen much, though."

I want the readers of this book to feel they could talk to me whenever they wanted to. As for the ideas in this book, you, of course, will pick and choose what might help you and reject the rest. In any event, I want to remain available.

Just send me a message to my email address at brian@brianmorganbooks.com. I'd love to hear from you.

I also have a website www.brianmorganbooks.com, and I'm also available on LinkedIn (as brianmorganbooks) and Facebook (as morganthewriter). If we connect, we can communicate through messaging.

Just let me know you read this book so I will know how we crossed tracks.

Thank you for reading my book.

Brian

About the author

Brian Morgan has won numerous state and national awards as a journalist, editor and author. His most prestigious national book award was the Fellowship of Australian Writers' National Literary Award, The Jim Hamilton Award.

In 2018, he received a special international accolade when he was designated as a Global Goodwill Ambassador as recognition of his lifetime of service to causes of human need. GGAs are pledged to work for the United Nations' Sustainable Development Goals for Human Rights.

Brian has also received local, state and national awards for community service. He has been described as a business and thought leader, a business founder, an integrity advocate and a voice for the unheard. He founded and ran Professional Independent Publishing Standards (PiPS) from 2014 to 2018.

His first book, published traditionally, was a sellout best-seller in the US and the UK, and his work has been translated for Vietnamese, Chinese and Japanese readers.

Brian now has ten books still available in print, all published independently through The Writers Trust, and he has helped other writers publish. All going well, several books are in line for publication in and beyond 2020.

More details are available on the author's website and on LinkedIn, Facebook, and other Internet sites.

Brian believes that a writer's life should be a life of service, a life of purpose. That is what drives him.

Where to find Brian Morgan's books

Details of all titles, including descriptions and reviews, can be found on the author's website www.brianmorganbooks.com. Details are also on your nation's Amazon site.

After the Storm:
A Better Life Beyond COVID

Live to Write:
Survive the Solitude - and Thrive

The Life of Jude:
Saint of the Impossible

The True Christmas Spirit:
Let Peace and Joy Fill Your Heart

The Broth of Oblivion:
A True Story of a Mother and her Dementia

The Saint of the Impossible:
Everything you wanted to know about Saint Jude

Save the Dreaming:
A Simple Plan to Rescue Aboriginal Culture

The Legend of the Magi Scrolls:
Timeless Christmas Classics

You Are Already Rich:
Riches Beyond Your Dreams,
Treasure Beyond Your Imaginings

The Richest Man in Persia:
This long-awaited sequel to The Richest Man in Babylon is today's blueprint for safe, ethical wealth and personal success.

To find a book, simply go to your Amazon website, go to the Books section and type in the full name of the book (main title and sub-title).
Thank you for your interest.

www.ingramcontent.com/pod-product-compliance
Lightning Source LLC
LaVergne TN
LVHW020628100826
845148LV00012B/2091

9780648514718